D1824311

Equalities and Inequalities in the English Education System

To Lucas, Robin, and Jake Scott

Equalities and Inequalities in the English Education System

David Scott and Ben Scott

 is an imprint of

First published in 2018 by the UCL Institute of Education Press, 20 Bedford Way, London WC1H 0AL

www.ucl-ioe-press.com

©2018 David Scott and Ben Scott

British Library Cataloguing in Publication Data:
A catalogue record for this publication is available from the British Library

ISBNs
978-1-85856-827-0 (paperback)
978-1-85856-866-9 (PDF eBook)
978-1-85856-867-6 (ePub eBook)
978-1-85856-868-3 (Kindle eBook)

All rights reserved. No part of this publication may be reproduced, stored in a retrieval system, or transmitted in any form or by any means, electronic, mechanical, photocopying, recording or otherwise, without the prior permission of the copyright owner.

Every effort has been made to trace copyright holders and to obtain their permission for the use of copyright material. The publisher apologizes for any errors or omissions and would be grateful if notified of any corrections that should be incorporated in future reprints or editions of this book.

The opinions expressed in this publication are those of the authors and do not necessarily reflect the views of the UCL Institute of Education.

Typeset by Quadrant Infotech (India) Pvt Ltd
Printed by CPI Group (UK) Ltd, Croydon, CR0 4YY
Cover image ©Brain light/Alamy Stock Photo

Images on pages 20–1
Apartheid in South Africa, ©Suretha Rous/Alamy Stock Photo
Characteristics of mouths, from *New Physiognomy* by Samuel R. Wells, 1894
Milan – Piazza Sant'Alessandro, reproduced by kind permission of Alessia Cross
Female Spanish Civil War fighters, 1937, photograph by Gerda Taro

Contents

List of tables, boxes, figures and images   viii

Preface   x

About the authors   xi

1. Introduction: Equality and inequality models   1

2. Private education   31

3. Teacher training   44

4. Selection and de-selection   59

5. Examination and testing   88

6. Divisions and demarcations: Dis-ability and sexuality   106

7. Inclusion and exclusion: Educational practices   127

References   148

Index   156

List of tables, boxes, figures and images

Tables

Table 2.1: Full-time pupils in independent schools, 1974–2016

Table 2.2: Types of school in the independent sector, 2017

Table 2.3: Gender and schools in the independent sector, 2017

Table 2.4: Day/boarding schools in the independent sector, 2017

Table 2.5: Destinations of 18-year-olds from the independent education sector, 2017

Table 2.6: Percentage of MPs educated in independent schools, 1979–2015

Table 2.7: Educational backgrounds in influential social groups, 2015

Table 4.1: Social class representation in admissions to grammar schools, 1900–39

Table 4.2: Number of maintained grammar schools and pupils, 1947–2016

Table 4.3: Pupil characteristics by selected school type, January 2016

Table 4.4: Summary of GCSE achievement by mainstream school type, 2014/15

Table 4.5: Mainstream state-funded faith schools in England by type, 2016

Table 4.6: Religious character of schools, 2016

Table 4.7: Primary, secondary, and all-age pupil numbers: schools in England, 2006–16

Table 4.8: Pupil numbers in state-funded schools in England, 2016

Table 4.9: School and pupil numbers by academy type, England, 2016

Table 5.1: UK placement in PISA league tables, 2015

Table 6.1: Pupils with special educational needs, England, 2007–16

Table 6.2: Pupils on SEN support or with a statement or EHC plan by type of need, England, 2016

Table 6.3: Types of provision attended by pupils with a statement or EHC plan, England, 2010–16

Boxes

Box 4.1:   Arithmetic test, 1910 (selected examples)
Box 4.2:   English grammar and composition, 1910 (selected examples)
Box 4.3:   Arithmetic entrance paper, 1933
Box 4.4:   English examinations, 1928–32: A selection of questions
Box 4.5:   Kent eleven-plus test: Specimen questions

Figures

Figure 1.1:   Changes over time to the percentage of income held by the top 10 per cent in four countries
Figure 1.2:   Inequality rates in the UK, 1979–2015
Figure 4.1:   Grammar school areas and groupings, England, 1998

Images on pages 20–1

Apartheid in South Africa
Characteristics of mouths, from *New Physiognomy* by Samuel R. Wells
Milan – Piazza Sant'Alessandro
Female Spanish Civil War fighters

Preface

There have recently been calls to adopt approaches to the study of the social world that deny the need to address ontological and epistemological issues. Advocates for these approaches give the impression that they are operating outside of and in opposition to philosophical framings concerning the nature of the world and how it can be known. They are being disingenuous, since reality, as we know it, is always concept-dependent. Their purpose is to support and strengthen a particular ideological view of human behaviour, which favours those forms of research and judgement that can be described as empiricist and technicist. Ontological and epistemological beliefs, then, underpin the development and use of strategies and methods by empirical researchers. In contrast, proponents of a pragmatic position, using this term in its ordinary language sense, argue that it is possible to separate out these beliefs from the adoption of methods and strategies. These methods and strategies are determined by how useful they are, and even by whether they are fit for purpose. This is not a coherent position to take.

Knowledge about, for example, the social categories of gender, race, dis-ability, intelligence, sexuality, and class is always framed by sets of ideas and moral ordinances, and as a consequence should not be treated unproblematically, as it frequently is by politicians, journalists, and many academics, not least in the field of education. This is what this book is about. It is an exercise in knowledge development, and it seeks to shed a modest amount of light on the workings of these social categories, because it seems to us that a proper examination of these is an essential starting point for understanding how equalities and inequalities are formed and how they operate in modern England.

Nothing here in this book proscribes a social dimension to the development of knowledge, and in turn our contention is that this dimension has to be carefully recorded by those committed to some form of truthful enquiry. Research, which is the principal mechanism for knowledge development, is both descriptive (understood in a non-representationalist way) *and* developmental and prescriptive; that is, it both gives an account of reality and in the process changes the nature of that reality, though not in every instance. It redescribes and reformulates the object of the investigation, and in some cases this is quite clearly its intention. It is incumbent on us, however, to treat all knowledge development as work in progress, as the philosopher Karl Popper was inclined to do.

David Scott and Ben Scott
20 June 2017

About the authors

David Scott is Emeritus Professor of Curriculum, Pedagogy and Assessment at the UCL Institute of Education, University College London. His most recent books are: Scott, D. (2016) *Education Systems and Learners: Knowledge and Knowers*; Scott, D., Husbands, C., Slee, R., Wilkins, R. and Terano, M. (2015) *Policy Transfer and Educational Change*; Scott, D. (2015) *Roy Bhaskar: A Theory of Education*; Scott, D. (2015) *New Perspectives on Curriculum, Pedagogy and Assessment*; and Scott, D. and Hargreaves, E. (eds) (2015) *Sage Handbook on Learning*. He has completed a large number of research projects in curriculum, pedagogy, and assessment.

Ben Scott is an independent educational consultant, who specializes in curriculum, assessment, and learning issues.

Chapter 1

Introduction: Equality and inequality models

When Donald Trump claimed during his ultimately successful campaign for election as president of the United States that his predecessor, Barack Obama, 'is the founder' of Islamic State and that Hillary Clinton, the Democratic candidate for the presidency, was the 'co-founder', some argued that this was a direct lie and an example of post-truth politics. Surely Trump didn't mean that literally? Perhaps what he meant was that the Obama administration's rapid withdrawal from Iraq created a vacuum that the terrorists then filled, so that by his actions he contributed to the formation of the Islamic State. However, Trump was not happy at this interpretation of his words: 'No, I meant he's the founder of Islamic State, he was the most valuable player. I give him the most valuable player award. I give her, too, by the way, Hillary Clinton.' When it was suggested that Obama was not sympathetic to the aims and purposes of Islamic State, Trump refused even to countenance this: 'I don't care. He was the founder. The way he got out of Iraq was, that, that was the founding of Islamic State, OK?' For Trump, this was the truth of the matter (*The Economist*, 10 September 2016).

During the campaign, Trump frequently made false conspiracy claims, such as Barack Obama's birthplace being outside the geographical area of the United States, and about the origins of birtherism. He claimed that the father of one of his rivals for the Republican presidential nomination, Ted Cruz, met with John F. Kennedy's assassin shortly before Lee Harvey Oswald murdered the president. Then there were claims, which he supported, about Muslims who cheered the 11 September 2001 attacks on New York and Washington, about vaccines that caused autism, about unreported explosives at the home of the San Bernardino terrorists, and antisemitism-tinged accounts of plots by bankers and the media. The point is not that Trump said these things; it is that he was able to persuade a large number of people that he was telling the truth.

During the election campaign a tape was released showing Trump boasting about sexually assaulting women. When a journalist, Megyn Kelly, asked about his treatment of women, Trump replied that he had 'no respect for her as a journalist' and alleged she had 'blood coming out of her nose, blood coming out of her wherever'. He personally targeted one of his Republican primary opponents, Carly Fiorina, by saying 'look at that face, would anybody vote for that?'. He tweeted that the wife of another of his Republican rivals, Ted Cruz, was less attractive than his own wife, Melania, and that Jeb Bush, yet another Republican presidential candidate, was sympathetic to illegal immigrants because his wife was of Mexican heritage. These were, in the main, just insults; but they were also attempts to frame the debate about gendered relations, with regard both to how they can be understood and to what is acceptable in society.

This book is about social categories such as gender, race, dis-ability, intelligence, sexuality, and class, as they are used in the field of education. (There are many more, but these are the principal ones.) Knowledge of and about them and their effects is central to how we can understand society, equalities and inequalities within it, and educational relations. Our intention here is to go beyond the surface meaning of these social categories, in contrast to many politicians who separate out facts from values without giving much thought to this relationship; or to journalists who refuse to accept that their carefully managed accounts of events and happenings in the world are always ideologically framed both in relation to their content and to how they are presented; or of course, to many academics, whose brand of knowledge is both dangerously reductive and philosophically naïve. So, for example, some argue that the knowledge frame for any claim about the world and therefore for whether that claim is true or not has to be reduced to concepts and the relations between them that can subsequently be measured; or that it is not possible to judge between different and rival theories about the same social object.

In our search for the truth, we can perhaps find some respite in the absolutely true meaning of words. If we are interested in the meaning of a word, we can look it up in a dictionary. So we can take a word such as 'truth' and come to a first set of definitions: 'the quality or state of being true', 'that which is true or in accordance with fact or reality', and 'a fact or belief that is accepted as true' (Dictionary.com, n.d.). We might then wonder what being 'in accordance with fact or reality' might be, and so we might look up the meaning of this phrase and find out that a 'fact' is 'a thing that is known or proved to be true', and 'information that is used as evidence or as part of a report or news article', and even information 'used to refer to a particular situation under discussion'. The first of these simply takes us back to where we started: truth is understood as being in accord with a fact or reality, and a fact is being defined now as a thing that is known or believed to be true. Our search for the truth about truth has stalled. We are further troubled by the word 'evidence', since we are told that a fact is used as evidence for important purposes. Once again we go back to our dictionary and find that 'evidence' is defined as 'the available body of facts or information indicating whether a belief or proposition is true or valid'. We are back to where we started and no further forward.

In addition, words can contain multiple meanings. For example, a notion such as objectivity, a key term in post-truth discursive politics, contains multiple rather than singular meanings, as it is used in the world. It is possible to give six different meanings to the word: namely, that something can exist objectively without it being perceived by human beings, that if something meets a set of truth conditions it is objective, that something is objective when the relevant knowers' traces (such as values and interests) are excluded, that something is objective if it can be directly accessed through observation, that something is objective if its mode of application to the world is correct, and that something is objective when more than one knower can agree on its truthfulness (Scott, 2011).

Does this mean that determining the truth is always a flawed enterprise? It would seem so. However, what we can say is that statements made by Trump and others are becoming more detached from the reality of our lives as we understand them and conform less to the accepted ways of how we can access the world. In other words, the purveyors of these post-factual truths are, knowingly or otherwise, creating a divide between the established and generally accepted (in particular societies) ways of establishing truths (usually about important issues in society such as the social categories) and the means (usually implicit) by which people come to believe certain things; although, of course, they might also be changing the rules of the game. And further to this, what quite clearly is also the case is that established ways and means of accepting truthful statements are subject to the contingencies of history. They change over time.

We can see this most clearly in relation to certain key concepts, for example race. The concept of race can signify a division of people into different groups. (This is only one way it can be used.) Under this conception, races are said to have some type of biological foundation, and this generates discrete racial groupings, so that members of each group share a set of biological characteristics that are not shared by members of other groups. These characteristics are inherited from other members of the same racial grouping; it therefore becomes possible to identify the geographical origin of each race. These inherited characteristics are usually thought of as physical phenotypes, such as hair colour, skin colour, eye shape, and bone structure; however – and this is where it becomes much more complicated – sometimes these characteristics are used to refer to behavioural phenotypes such as intelligence or criminality. For example, in 1735 Carl Linnaeus divided human beings, *Homo sapiens*, into four distinct groupings – Europaeus, Asiaticus, Americanus, and Afer – and associated each of them with a different humour or personality type: sanguine, melancholic, choleric, and phlegmatic, respectively (Anderson, 2009). Indeed, he described the first of these groupings as 'active, acute and adventurous', and the last of these as 'crafty, lazy and careless'. James Watson, who, with Francis Crick, Rosalind Franklin, and Maurice Wilkins, discovered the double-helix structure of DNA, claimed in 2007 that black people were less intelligent than white people and that the idea of all racial groups sharing common and equal powers of reason was a delusion (Rutherford, 2014). It is fairly easy to see that a belief in the concept of race as it is understood and defined here leads to certain social and political practices that discriminate against particular people, and in addition that categories such as race, and subsequently the development of social and pedagogical practices associated with them, are not fixed in an essentialist sense and can be changed. They are not natural kinds.

And this is why Trump's rhetoric is so dangerous. Essentializing the categories (i.e. gender, race, dis-ability, intelligence, sexuality, and class) and doing so in a way that privileges one grouping at the expense of another or set of others is a manifestation of the post-truth politics being played out. However, not all is lost. A number of arguments can be and have been put forward to attempt to explain why one theory is better than another, and indeed whether one of these theories is more truthful than another. This has been done in relation, for example, to the claims made about birtherism or the causes of autism. The first of these is that there are real issues that impact on our lives and it is these real issues that determine the truthfulness of particular theories. What this indicates, even if it is not an entirely satisfactory solution to our problem, is that one of our criteria for this determination is the referent of knowledge (indeed, that knowledge does have a referent). This is an important step in the argument for deciding that one theory is better than another, or that this or that claim regarding gendered relations or economic differences between rich and poor people, for example, is true or false.

The most promising argument in favour of being able to distinguish between true and false claims is that there has to be a relation or connection between knowledge development and the world (not of course in a correspondence or representational sense). This argument rests on the foundational claim that knowledge is not the same as and is different in some important respects from what it claims to be about, that is, its referent, and in addition that it then becomes possible to produce knowledge of this connection or relation and of the world itself, even if it is indirect. If we can show how the process might work, then we can initiate the activity of grounding our theories in the world as it is and thus establishing in part the truth-capacity of claiming that one theory is better than another. This is the epistemic claim, where accounts of the world are more truthful because they have a better relationship with and to the world. However, this can only be established retroductively; that is, there is a process involved in knowing the world: sensate experience only takes us so far. Retroductive processes comprise the fashioning of inferential connections between mind and world, and therefore constitute moves that take us from a description and analysis of particular experiential accounts of the world to a reconstruction of the basic conditions for these phenomena to be as they are. This is a long and arduous process, and one, moreover, in which politicians, journalists, and most of the research community choose not to engage.

Another argument is that if a claim about the world can explain more significant phenomena than another then it is a superior theory. Clearly, if there are anomalies, contradictions, or inadequacies in a theory or claim, then we can argue that this theory or claim is false. So in trying to determine whether it is possible to determine that a theory is superior to another theory then we also (in addition to our epistemic criterion) have to build in a notion of rational adequacy.

How then do we differentiate between truth and falsehood? There are four ways of distinguishing between different theories or models of, for example, these striations in the social landscape, that is, the categories we listed earlier. The first is epistemic, so that a theory is superior to another because it is more empirically adequate and thus is more truthful. The second is the converse, so that a version of reality is superior to another because it contains fewer contradictions, disjunctions, and errors. A third approach focuses on the giving of reasons, and concludes that some reasons and systems of rationality are superior to others, and therefore should be preferred. A fourth approach is pragmatic: a theory is better than another because it is more practically adequate or referenced to/part of extant frameworks of meaning. A combination of all four reasons is, we suggest, appropriate. And this allows us to distinguish truth from falsehood.

The structuring of the discourse

This refers to the truth or otherwise of different and powerful discourses about striations in the social landscape, such as gender, race, dis-ability, intelligence, sexuality, and class. There are others of course, such as religious affiliation, but in this book we will be dealing principally with these six striations and the divisions and differences they create in modern societies. A discourse is a set of propositions about the world joined together by a set of connectives and relations that offers an account of an object or objects in the world, and may even act to create objects in the world. It can have a material form, that is, it can be written, orally presented, or stored electronically as text, and it is usually mediated through a language or languages. Implicit within every discursive formation are a number of features: a propositional account of a person, including their emergent capacities and affordances, and the environment within which they are situated; a propositional account of the relationship between a person and their environment; propositional knowledge about understanding, learning, and change, with regard to the person and the environments in which they are located; inferences from these premises and conclusions about appropriate representations, media for representations, and learning environments; and a set of practical actions that emanate from these claims. However, what needs to be said time and time again is that a discursive construction can never be a simple determinant of identity, behaviour, or action. Discourses are structured in a variety of ways, and both this meta-structuring and the forms it produces are relative to time and place. These meta-forms refer to constructs such as generality, balance of performativity and denotation, relative value, hierarchical binary opposition, representation, and legitimacy.

The first of these is the designation of objects as separate from other objects in the world. In part, this constitutes a naming process and it refers to the relations between singulars and generalities: in other words, to that which constitutes those items within a general description of a set of objects, such as male/female, abled/dis-abled, black/white, heterosexual/homosexual, cognitive ability/cognitive disability, and socio-economic advantage/socio-economic disadvantage.

A second meta-form concerns the balance in educational and social statements between denotation and performativity, or between offering an account of something with no intention of changing the world and offering an account which is intended to change an object or create a new one. Trumpian rhetoric certainly seems to subscribe to the latter rather than the former, and is therefore performative in so far as the utterer (male in this case) is not intending to merely describe what he thinks is in the world; rather, in making the statement, he intends to bring something into being. There is of course no guarantee that performative statements will in fact achieve their purpose. Denotative statements have a different function, in that they seek to describe what currently exists, what might exist in the future, and what has happened in the past. The intention of the utterer is not to bring anything into being in the world. This distinction between performativity and denotation only makes sense in terms of the intentionality of the maker of the utterance and in terms of the perceived relationship between statement and act; in other words, it implies such a relationship exists even if it does not specify what that relationship is. Educational and social statements in relation to the categories then may be characterized in terms of the balance of performativity and denotation within them.

A third meta-epistemic form concerns the relative value given to an object in comparison with another object. For example, within a race discourse one of the pair of words is given a greater value than the other, with a fairly obvious example being that white is privileged over black. In a gendered discourse, male is given a more important valuation than female. Dis-ability is understood as inferior to ability, and so on.

The fourth meta-structuring device refers to the bipolarity of objects, descriptions and dispositions, or hierarchically binary oppositions; that is, an object, description, or disposition is defined in terms of another object, description, or disposition of which it is the mirror opposite. If the male/female binary is used as an example, it is possible to see that the positioning of the two terms as oppositional in meaning, and the subsequent valuing of one (male) and the devaluing of the other (female) because of their oppositionality, has significant implications for the way the debate about relations between the two concepts can be conducted. Thus certain words, phrases, descriptors, and concepts are understood in bipolar terms, which determine how they can be used as a resource for understanding the world.

A fifth meta-principle refers to the referential value of a statement. Making an educational or social statement implies that a particular type of truth-value is being invoked. So, for example, a correspondence theory represents the truth of whether the statement mirrors the reality that it seeks to describe. A number of such theories are in existence, some fairly primitive (such as naïve appeals to facts), others more sophisticated (so that they avoid mirror imagery and at least take account of sceptical arguments). On the other hand, coherence theories argue that the truth-value of a statement lies not in its reference to an external world but in whether it fits coherently in a web of knowledge. An educational statement about one or more of the categories therefore implicitly or explicitly is underpinned by a theory of reference embedded within a theory of truth, and this marks it out as a knowledge form.

A sixth meta-principle refers to the way in which the particular ideas, concepts, phrases, and descriptors are embedded in networks of ideas, concepts, phrases, and descriptors, and have a history. So, for example, race as a concept is always positioned in a bewilderingly complicated network of other terms, such as innateness, trait theory, genetics, phenotypicality, biology, historical origin, evolutionary theory, and many more.

We have been referring here to the relations in the discourse between different ideas and notions, and how these can vary depending on the discourse. These relations are those of generality, balance of performativity and denotation, relative value, hierarchical binary opposition, representation, and legitimacy (Scott, 2017). Each of these in turn can vary in relation to any of the others. Societies are different because different valuations are given to each of them. These valuations then determine how we can understand the six important categories that concern us in this book: gender, race, dis-ability, intelligence, sexuality, and class.

Gender

An important binary that has had real effects is the male/female binary, an oppositional coupling of two words or phrases, and this implies a relationship between these two descriptive terms, both of which can be problematized. In addition, the strength, type, and probative force of this relationship is crucial to the discourse that is in operation. We therefore need to examine in the first instance the principal characteristics of this male/female dyad. Initially we will focus on the critique that radical feminists make of traditional conceptions of what constitutes true or valid knowledge about the world. Although women have been actively involved throughout the centuries in building societies, they have been marginalized when it comes to the production of knowledge about societies and social activity. Feminists therefore ask how epistemological categories are implicated in defining masculinity and femininity, how they function to define the nature of people, how they work to attach different valuations to their skills and capacities, and how gender difference is a category of analysis around which every society is structured.

These questions about how knowledge is produced and who is involved in that production underpin all discussions about particular sets of categories. They lead to a questioning of the analytic categories that are taken for granted, and in particular of how these structure outlooks and dispositions and provide the criteria for evaluating social experience.

Feminist theory is not a unified or homogeneous set of ideas but rather encompasses a variety of different perspectives and approaches. Liberal feminism is widely represented in the contemporary Euro-American world. Since the 1960s, the relationship between liberalism and feminism has underpinned the equal opportunities paradigm so influential in education and social policy. The emphasis is on removing barriers to women's participation in all aspects of public life and arguing for a greater share for women in the rights, privileges, and opportunities enjoyed by men. This variety of feminism is founded on the emancipatory impulse of liberalism, itself a significant aspect of Enlightenment thought. Its key elements are a belief in an inherent human nature, a commitment to progress, and a trust in rationality. Liberal feminism espouses an egalitarian politics, arguing that if men and women are treated equally in political, social, and personal terms, then women's views and activities would be invested with the same degree of significance as men's. What prevents this is the fact of female subordination and oppression. This can be best understood as a problem of sexism, defined as the unwarranted differential treatment of women, which can be identified empirically and eradicated through appropriate policies and programmes.

By the 1980s feminists were attempting to integrate their approaches into mainstream critical theories such as neo-Marxism (e.g. hooks, 1982). These feminists argued that gender inequality derives from capitalism and that men's domination over women is a by-product of capital's domination of labour. Class is regarded as the fundamental category of social structure, and gender difference and inequality as a secondary feature of the economic exploitation practised through the control of one class over another. The site of women's exploitation is sometimes argued to be the family, whilst the focus is on the ideological rather than the material relations of capitalism.

A number of feminists from both conservative and radical positions have united around a position that advocates the privileging of traditional 'feminine' values (see Daly, 1992). They accept the view that women's 'nature' is different from men's and that women excel in relational and nurturing practices. Radical feminists then argue that if rationality is associated with domination and control of the natural world, with all its destructive implications, then women are fortunate not to be associated with it. They go on to argue that the characteristics associated with femininity, such as caring, relatedness, and community, should therefore be valorized over male characteristics. In other words, they all, irrespective of emphasis, accept the rational/irrational binary and its association with masculine/feminine difference, arguing simply that the hierarchy should be reversed, with a consequent privileging of all aspects of the feminine over the masculine.

By the 1980s many feminists had become disillusioned with the political project of making women equal to men. They found mainstream discourses particularly resistant to their challenge, or incapable of being broadened to include women. These experiences of being rejected and alienated led to a growing awareness of the deep-rooted patriarchal nature of such discourses. Even if sexism was eliminated, with both sexes participating fully, the patriarchal nature of structures and value systems would still ensure that men and women were positioned unequally in terms of power, with female experience still defined as marginal and of lesser significance to male experience. Even if women were to be incorporated into patriarchal discourses, it would be on the basis of their sameness to men, their specificity as women not being acknowledged. In other words, women had to become surrogate men. The development of a more radical feminism therefore was a response to the perceived limitations of other approaches, which, it was argued, were based on irresolvable contradictions within which women could not escape an inferior definition and an unequal positioning.

In radical feminism (e.g. Griffin, 2000; Flax, 1990), the focus shifts from equal opportunities to the phallocentric nature of all systems of representation; to the observation that whenever the two sexes are represented in a single model, the feminine is always collapsed into a universal model represented in masculine terms. At the theoretical level, feminists have analysed how the general concepts, assumptions, and categories of Western thought have been organized around hierarchies, which by association privilege masculinity and devalue femininity. Regardless of which academic discipline radical feminists are working within, there is a widespread recognition that epistemological issues do not exist in a social vacuum but rather exert a powerful influence on concepts, ideals, and values. The way we make sense of the world is through broad categories and central questions to do with the nature of reality, subjectivity, knowledge-construction, morality and ethics, and political rights and responsibilities. The development of feminist theory has stimulated questions about how philosophy is implicated in defining masculinity and femininity, how it defines the 'nature' of people, the values attached to their skills and capacities, and how gender difference is a central analytic category around which every society is structured.

Radical feminists have added the insight that when notions such as rationality, knowledge, and the self are deconstructed, their gendered nature is revealed, so that concepts which have been taken as neutral and universal are shown in effect to be masculine. The privileging of the rational is at the heart of modernist epistemology, yet this is a form of rationality that itself privileges the masculine. The claim of empirical/analytic epistemology – that rationality, objectivity, and abstraction are the only guarantees of truth – is actually a specifically masculine claim. Furthermore, each of the oppositions that structures modernist thought is derivative of the most fundamental opposition of all, that of masculine/feminine, male/female. In all binaries the male is associated with the first element, the female with the second. In each case the male element is privileged over the female and maintains its position by its capacity to define itself as a universal norm against which the subjective, the emotional, the aesthetic, the natural, and above all the feminine, are judged and found wanting. Thus through the very dualities of modernist thought, women's significance is defined as inferior to the rational, objective, abstract qualities of scientific method, which not only guarantees truth but positions masculinity and 'man' as a legitimate knower, capable of discovering truth. Once this kind of analysis is accepted, all the other common-sense stereotypes about gendered identities, which feminists attempt to counter, fall into perspective.

Essentialists try to exalt the virtues of female nature and related notions of community, caring, and relatedness, as opposed to the male virtues of control, mastery, abstraction, and rationality. But these arguments are unconvincing because they have not challenged the very opposition through which the female is defined as inferior in the first place, and hence they cannot succeed in privileging the female over the male. 'Equal but different' simply cannot succeed in a world where knowledge is constructed hierarchically. What emerges therefore is that if particular binaries are not reversed and ultimately dissolved, oppressive structures of thought and knowledge will continue to exert their power.

All varieties of feminism try to show how gender relations operate in favour of male hegemony, and their aim is to help effect a redistribution of power towards women. This may often imply the writing of histories or giving expression to voices and views that have been suppressed or denied. Models of investigation which assume homogeneity or an 'economy of the same' as their starting point fail to acknowledge difference and insist that women can be represented as having the same characteristics as men. However, there is also the implication that not all women have some universal experience that can serve as a standpoint for the building of feminist theory and practice. The category 'woman' is not unified; women's experience is differentiated through such factors as class, ethnicity, race, religion, and many others. This means that our understanding needs to be sensitive to this diversity of female experience and for the power relations that are present among women.

Race categories

Determining the boundaries between different racial groupings has proved to be somewhat controversial, and self-evidently these racial groupings, whether real or constructed, have had powerful effects. One form that these racial groupings took was that there are only four distinct races, each both geographically based and allied with a phenotype of skin colour: white or Caucasian, black or African, yellow or Asian, and red or North American (Anemone, 2011). This categorization downplayed other biological or phenotypical distinctions, reduced all human beings to four basic categories, and identified skin colour as the determining factor in race and racial categorizations. Within this system, no distinction was made between, for example, Scandinavians and Italians, both categories being subsumed into the white or Caucasian category. Other taxonomists tried to distinguish between Nordic, Alpine, and Mediterranean races, but with little success.

The difficulties that these taxonomists encountered led to a belief that race as a category was socially constructed, and not just through the nominalization process itself or through biology. However, some biologists persisted in their belief in racial categories, arguing that reproductive isolation during human evolution or through social practices such as miscegenation had led to the existence of different groups of human beings sharing physical phenotypes and even to clusters of genetic material. In addition, some argued for the formation of socially constructed and differentiated racial categories. All of these different viewpoints pointed to and indeed encouraged the idea that these different racial groups can be unequally valued in society. Theoretical frameworks such as racial formation theory (e.g. Omi and Winant, 1994) and critical race theory (e.g. Ladson-Billings and Tate, 1995) explore the implications of treating race as a social construction by examining the images, narratives, and ideas of race as they play out in everyday life.

Dis-ability

The underpinning philosophy of inclusive education systems has in the past drawn on two dominant and contradictory models of disability, namely the medical and social models. Generally, advocates of special education and integration support the medical model, while purists of inclusion favour the social model of disability. While the medical model suggests that problems and differences lie with the individual, the social model places the emphasis on socio-economic and cultural factors.

Examples of socio-economic factors are poor nutrition or contaminated water, while cultural factors refer to the ideological construction of the notion of disability or difference. For example, the language used in a specific culture for disability or disadvantage indicates what is considered to be normal or abnormal in that culture. From this perspective, the focus of the medical model is on biology, which points to a physical treatment for disability and difference. In contrast, in adopting a social model, the emphasis is placed on addressing social barriers to inclusion, such as placing ramps in the streets to help people with disabilities move around. Additionally, from a cultural point of view, the emphasis is on the need to transform the attitudes adopted in relation to, and the language used about, disability and difference, because it impacts on how well people with disabilities or differences can be successfully included and represented in society.

In a critique of the dominant models of disability (i.e. medical, socio-economic, cultural) Bhaskar and Danermark (2006: 281) argue that 'each of these models accentuates just one of what are in fact a multiplicity of mechanisms involved in the formation and reproduction of disabilities'. For example, the social model has omitted the 'disabled body' from the discourse (Allan, 2008) by shifting the emphasis from the biological to the environmental. The medical model, in turn, has neglected environmental factors by foregrounding the 'disabled body'. Recent research on disability encourages a more holistic approach and emphasizes all the different levels of reality. Inclusive education is consequently understood as a socio-economic, political, embodied, personal, and cultural matter.

Intelligence

Learners are constructed pedagogically. An example of this process is the application of the notion of intelligence, and in particular the use of the idea of a fixed, innate quality in human beings which can be measured and remains relatively stable throughout an individual's life. This has come to be known as an intelligence quotient and is measured by various forms of testing, for example the eleven-plus test. The eleven-plus had a significant influence on the formation of the tripartite system of formal education in the UK in 1944 as it was used to classify children as appropriate candidates for grammar schools (if they passed the eleven-plus), technical schools (if they passed the eleven-plus but were considered to be better suited to receive a technical education), and secondary moderns (if, like the vast majority, they failed the eleven-plus and would, in the early days of the tripartite system, leave school without any formal qualifications). This system of education was later largely replaced by a comprehensive system of schooling. At the time of writing this book, the Conservative government in the UK looks set to reintroduce the eleven-plus examination, grammar schools, and secondary moderns into the system.

This illustrates one of the problems with an approach to the relationship between mind and reality that is technicist, scientistic, and reductionist. What was considered to be a natural kind, that is, innate qualities of intelligence in human beings, has been shown to have undeniably social or constructed dimensions to it. Powerful people have constructed a tool or apparatus for organizing educational provision, and given it credibility by suggesting that it was natural and thus had legitimacy. One manifestation of this discourse is the 'gifted and talented' programmes that have been introduced into schools in the UK over the last twenty years. 'Gifted and talented' is a term defined by the Department for Education in the UK to describe children who 'have the potential' to develop significantly beyond what is expected for their age. The suggestion by the Department for Education and others is that some children have this potential and others do not. It is also closely allied to processes of individualization and personalization that are becoming commonplace in UK educational settings, and has contributed to a sterility and impoverishment of learning approaches and outcomes in schools.

Central to the concept of the intelligence quotient is the tension between the relative emphasis given to genetically inherited characteristics and the influence of the environment. Many contemporary educationalists believe that children's early and continuing experiences at home and at school constitute the most significant influence on their intellectual achievement. However, early exponents of the argument that genetic inheritance determines intellectual potential saw intelligence, measured by tests, as a factor that could be isolated to produce a 'quotient' by which individuals could be classified. Regardless of environmental factors such as teaching and learning programmes or socio-economic variables, it was argued, some people were born with low levels of intelligence. Schooling could bring them to a certain level of achievement, but there would always be a ceiling imposed genetically on their capabilities. An extreme version of this belief was that intelligence, like certain physical characteristics, followed a normal curve of distribution, so that within any given population there were a set number of intelligent people and a set number of less intelligent people. It was further argued that those individuals who were most generously endowed were obviously more fitted to govern and take decisions on behalf of those who were less fortunate.

The use of IQ tests was widely accepted as a selective device among academics and the writers of government reports, including, for example, the Spens Report (1938) and the Norwood Report (1943), both of which influenced the writing of the UK Education Act of 1944. The 1944 Education Act incorporated the beliefs that intelligence testing could reliably predict who would succeed academically at a later point in time, and that children could and should be divided into categories based on the results and educated separately, though these principles weren't explicitly stated as such.

Soon after the 1944 Act was passed, the use of IQ tests to allocate places began to be discredited. One of the appeals of the policy was its supposed objectivity and reliability. If intelligence was innate and could be measured, then the tests would simply reflect this notionally 'pure' relationship – but this is not what happened. A number of other problems with this idealized concept became apparent. IQ tests should by definition be criterion referenced. If children had the intelligence, the theory went, then the tests would show it. All children who demonstrated their intelligence by achieving the designated mark ought to be awarded a place at a grammar school. In practice, local education authorities set quotas for grammar school entrance. Furthermore, different local education authorities set different quotas (Vernon, 1957). The quotas also discriminated against girls; the argument was frequently made that since girls developed earlier than boys in their intellectual abilities, fewer girls should be given places in grammar schools because this would discriminate unfairly against boys, who would catch up later.

A second problem with IQ tests was that if intelligence, as measured by the tests, was innate, then coaching and practice ought not to improve pupils' test scores. However, it was reported that pupils' performances were indeed enhanced by preparation for the tests, demonstrating that a supposedly freestanding assessment was being connected to the curriculum in contradiction to the intentions that lay behind it (Yates and Pidgeon, 1957). More importantly, Yates and Pidgeon's findings threw into question the notion of an innate and immutable intelligence quotient. Finally, the deterministic beliefs underlying the system implied low academic expectations for pupils who failed the eleven-plus. A low IQ score at 11 ought to be a reliable guide to the rest of a child's school career. However, it quickly became apparent that some of those who failed were capable of achieving high levels of academic success.

Sexuality

Ideas influence human practices, which means that both ideas and practices have histories. The contemporary division of heterosexual and homosexual terms made no sense to the ancient Greeks, although there were regional variations on understandings of sexuality. Same-sex relations, for example, were celebrated in some parts of Greece, whereas in parts of Ionia they were disapproved of. Physiological differences between the sexes were considered to be of less importance than beauty in either of the sexes. In *Erotikos* (Dialogue on Love) Plutarch argues that 'the noble lover of beauty engages in love wherever he sees excellence and splendid natural endowment without regard for any difference in physiological detail' (see Hayes and Nimis, 2011: 32). What was regarded as important was whether the person exercised moderation in their sexual dealings. In addition, status had a gendered and aged dimension, so that a freeman having sex with a woman or a boy was considered to be acceptable, but sexual relations between freemen were more problematic. The most important distinction was not physiological but the taking of active or penetrative roles as against passive or penetrated ones. The latter roles were only appropriate for social inferiors, such as women, slaves, and male youths.

The early period of the ancient Roman Republic had similar attitudes towards sexuality. With the formation of the Empire, attitudes began to change, even before Christianity became influential. There are few criticisms of same-sex relations in the Gospels; however, early Christian Church Fathers spoke out strongly against such relationships. Generally, though, the expression of sexuality and therefore in particular of same-sex sexuality was not considered to be sinful. With a greater emphasis placed on marriage (understood as taking place between two people differentiated by their reproductive capabilities) by such renowned scholars as St Augustine (Van der Meer, 1961), same-sex relations were prohibited and indeed in some parts of the now-Christian world attracted horrific punishments. For example, in Justinian's code of 529 AD, persons who were caught engaging in homosexual sex were executed, though different provisions applied to those who repented. This rise in intolerance towards certain types of sexual behaviour, that is, same-sex relations and sex outside of marriage, had important regional variations. As the Roman Empire weakened, to be replaced by a number of disparate barbarian kingdoms, a general tolerance towards both of these prevailed; and indeed, there were few legal prohibitions in Europe against homosexuality right up until the middle of the thirteenth century. All of this changed with the onset of the Gregorian reform movement in the Catholic Church, which argued for licensing natural kinds of sexuality and therefore for prohibiting unnatural kinds, such as homosexuality, extramarital sex, non-procreative sex within marriage, and sometimes even masturbation (Boswell, 1980).

This appeal to natural law became a defining feature of the spread of ideas concerning sexuality over the next six hundred years, and is only now beginning to be played out. However, we should be careful about these distinctions in the early and late medieval periods; for example, a 'sodomite' was understood in a different way from our modern conception of the notion of being a homosexual person (or even in some circumstances a heterosexual married person). It was not so much being of a certain sexual type but engaging in acts of a same-sex nature that was of concern. And in addition, if the person repented, then they could be excused punishments that were reserved for sodomites. Gender again was not decisive.

Despite the risk of severe punishment, homosexual cultures flourished in many European cities in the nineteenth century. In addition, there were significant reductions in legal penalties for sodomy (not just homosexuality), with the Napoleonic code decriminalizing it. However, there were moves, supported by new frameworks of ideas, to reinforce strong boundaries between the sexes, and this in turn meant that same-sex relations between people of roughly the same age became or at least were becoming the norm. Scientific accounts of sexuality at this time, based as they were on notions of mechanical causation, led to views of sexuality as biologically given or innate in the person. Medieval views that, for example, sodomy was freely chosen by the individual were giving way to ideas of the passive homosexual, and that as a consequence it became possible to portray homosexuality as defective or even pathological, with all the authority that the medical model could muster. In the twentieth century sexual roles were transformed. Premarital intercourse became an acceptable norm, as did the association of sex with pleasure, in opposition to some sections of the Catholic Church, which still understood sex as exclusively procreational. Gay sex became increasingly celebrated. The American Psychiatric Association removed homosexuality from its list of deviant sexual acts, and legal equality for gays and lesbians became permanent features of European and North American life.

Social class

Social class refers to a group of people with similar levels of wealth, influence, and status. The distinction between classes, that is, the economic category that ascribes a person to one class or another, is disputed: both in relation to belonging to a particular category and the inclusive nature of the category itself. Class has originally been understood as denoting different strata in society. Caste, an early form of class division at the time of the British Raj in India, can be understood as inclusive of the following: determination of particular caste membership by birth; a hierarchical system with the Brahmins at the head of the hierarchy; a segregation of society into more and less powerful groups; inter-group restrictions relating to mixing with other groups, though this didn't prevent forms of service whereby lower-caste members served higher-caste members; segregated geographical entities; and the development of rules and restrictions which allowed higher-caste members access and restricted the access of lower-caste members. Occupations were generally inherited and certain types of occupations were restricted to higher castes: for example, higher-caste members such as Brahmins and Kshatriyas became warriors and lower-caste members became agricultural workers. Restrictions were placed on inter-caste marriage. These rules and restrictions were sometimes relaxed at particular historical times and in different parts of India, often for economic reasons.

An original system of distinctions in the UK and much of Europe in medieval times concerned rank within the estate system of feudal and non-industrial societies. Distinctions were based on tradition and a complicated system of formal rights and duties. A more sophisticated class system emerged with the advent of industrialization and capitalist relations of production, whereby rank and status were gradually replaced by the criterion of material possessions. In the *Communist Manifesto*, Karl Marx and Friedrich Engels (2004) associated class with different relations to the means of production. Thus for Marx and Engels the criterion of class was economic. However, the problem with this notion of class is that it is difficult to find a single unambiguous criterion, whether it is occupation or a particular relation to the processes of production, that does not encounter logical and empirical difficulties. For example, how does one classify those who stand outside production and the productive process? For Max Weber (2013), class is a term that allows the identification of individuals with similar life chances in terms of opportunities for gaining resources. This refers to income and property acquisition, as well as skill, disposition, and cultural capitals. He understood the major historical struggle as being between creditors and debtors, with the conflict under capitalism between employers and workers as being a special case.

A more recent attempt at social class categorization identifies seven levels or strata, with this system being constructed by analysing people's income levels, assets, the professions of their peer group, and their social activities (Devine, 2004). At the very bottom is the precariat: this grouping typically consists of shopworkers, drivers, and cleaners. In the UK currently they represent about 15 per cent of the population and they lack any significant economic, cultural, and social capital. The everyday lives of this group of people are literally precarious. Above them are the traditional working class who, although they perform poorly in terms of the acquisition and retention of economic, cultural, and social capital, are not the poorest group – they are, though, the oldest. Above them is an emergent service workers' class, whose members have low levels of economic capital, but high levels of emerging cultural capital and high social capital. They are generally young and often found in urban areas. In the social class hierarchy at the next level are the technical middle classes. This is a new, small class with high levels of economic capital, low levels of cultural engagement, and relatively few social contacts. Above them are the new affluent workers, whose members have moderate levels of economic capital, but in contrast high levels of cultural and social capital. Then there are the established middle classes, whose members have high levels of economic, cultural, and social capital. They tend to be gregarious and culturally engaged. At the top of the system are the elite. This is the most privileged class, and its members have high levels of all three types of capital; this sets them apart to some extent. This classificatory system has similar faults to all the social class systems that have been put forward, in that it generalizes from individual lives to a limited number of groups and thus acts to reduce what is a complicated set of social relations to something which is manageable but not necessarily well-grounded.

Equalities and inequalities

Within each of these social categories – gender, race, dis-ability, intelligence, sexuality, and class – there is the potential for differences between members (i.e. higher and lower class members, or abled and dis-abled people); indeed, these differences are part of the various discourses emanating from the social categories. Social equalities are manifestations of weak boundaries between members of these social categories; social inequalities denote strong boundaries between them. In other words, notions of difference and different practices vary between different social, geographical, and historical environments (cf. the four images of difference on the following pages, which act as markers of position, place or route in relation to notions of difference or different practices – see p. vi for full image details).

Apartheid in South Africa

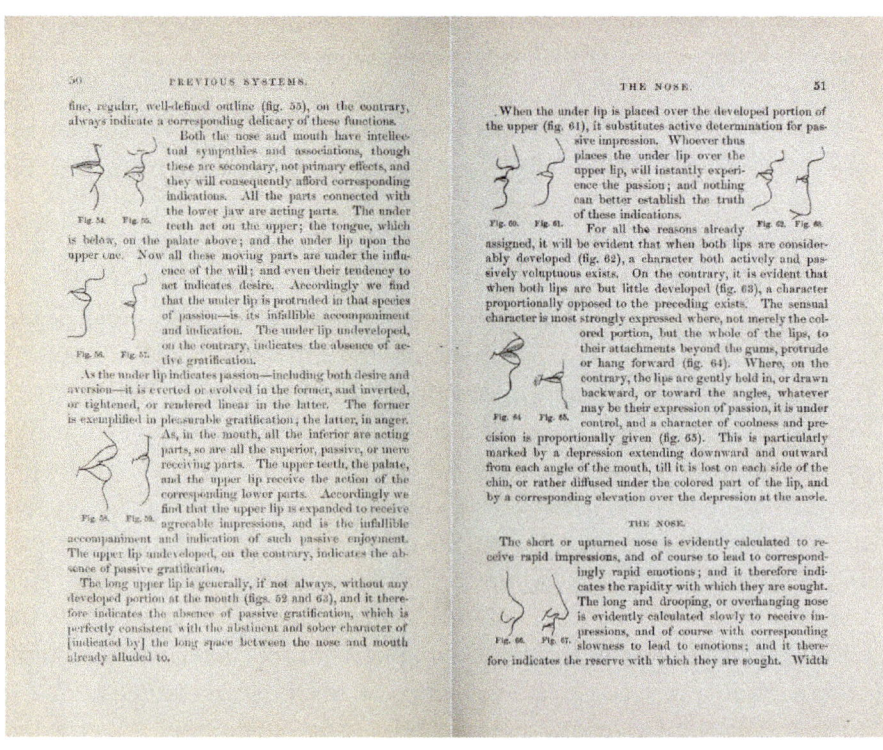

Characteristics of mouths, from *New Physiognomy* by Samuel R. Wells

Milan – Piazza Sant'Alessandro, reproduced by kind permission of Alessia Cross

Female Spanish Civil War fighters

In this book we will examine, at the empirical, actual, and real levels (cf. Bhaskar, 2011), three broad types of equality: equality of goods, equality of opportunity, and basic capability equality. Equality signifies some form of correspondence between a group of different objects, persons, or processes that have the same qualities in at least one respect, but not in every single feature. Inequality points to the opposite effect. Equality of goods suggests that an education system is equal when all the members of a society have equal access to what the system of education can offer, that is, the best curriculum, the best teaching, the best resources for learning, and so forth. Inequality of goods suggests that some members of that society are denied access to the best curricula, teaching, and resources in the system.

An example of inequalities of goods is the relative levels of income in different countries and how these have changed over time. Figure 1.1 compares levels of income inequality in the United States, France, Sweden, and Norway as to how the proportion of a country's wealth held by the top 10 per cent of the country changes over time. In the United States we can see that between 1920 and 1960 the amount of goods held by different groups became more equal. The trend since 1970, however, has been reversed, signifying an increasing divide in terms of the ownership of economic goods between the top 10 per cent and the rest of the population. However, in France, Norway, and Sweden, though the trend towards equality was similar to the United States between 1920 and 1960, in all three cases there was no reversal of this trend and these remain relatively equal societies (see Figure 1.1). Our remarks about inequalities and equalities here refer to only one element, that of economic goods, and not to other types of goods such as family support or education. In addition, it is possible to suggest that inequalities in the opportunities to acquire goods and inequalities in life conditions are also affected by pre-existing inequalities of goods.

Figure 1.1 compares the top 10 per cent of the population with the bottom 90 per cent of the population in these four countries. Figure 1.2 shows how inequality, as measured by the Gini coefficient for disposable household income, increased between 1979 and 2015 in the UK. This is a measure of inequality of goods.

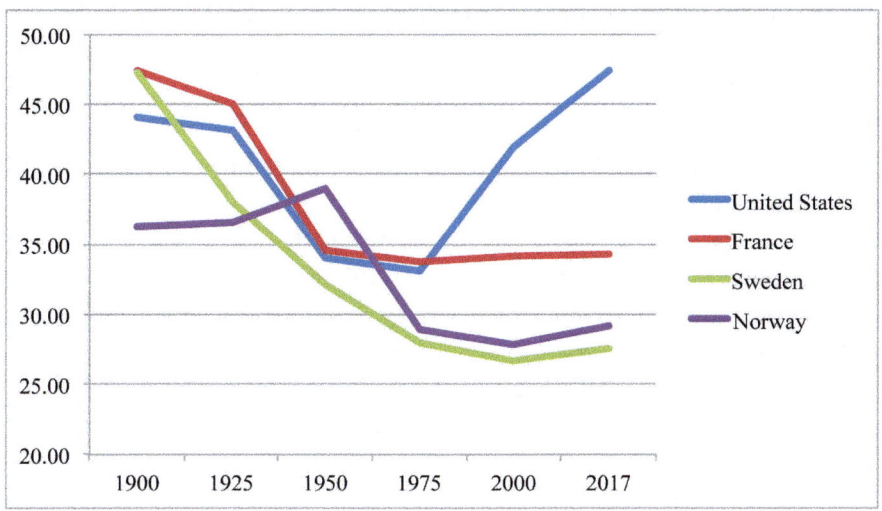

Figure 1.1: Changes over time to the percentage of income held by the top 10 per cent in four countries (United States, France, Sweden, and Norway)
Source: UNESCO (n.d.).

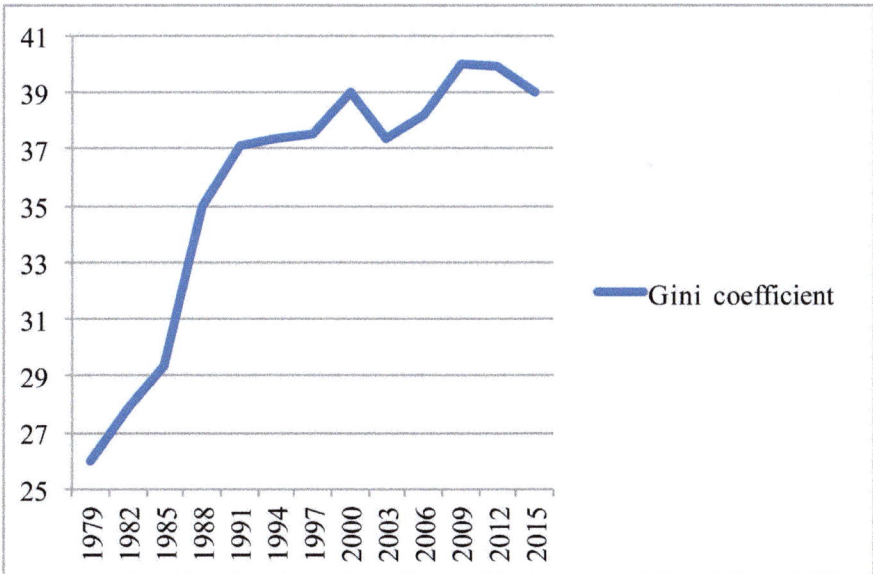

Figure 1.2: Inequality rates in the UK, 1979–2015: Households earning below average disposable income (millions)
Source: Office for National Statistics (2015).

Equality of opportunity is a political ideal that is opposed to hierarchy as an enduring feature of the society. The background assumption is that a society contains a hierarchy of more and less desirable, superior and inferior positions – or there may be several such hierarchies. In a class-based society, the assignment of individuals to places in the social hierarchy is fixed by birth. The child acquires the social status of his or her parents and the rewards that are associated with it. Social mobility may be possible in a class-based society, but the process whereby one is admitted to a different level of the hierarchy is open only to some individuals depending on their initial social status. In contrast, if there is an equality of opportunity, assigning individuals to places in the social hierarchy is determined by some form of competitive process, and all members of society are eligible to compete on equal terms.

Successive governments in the UK have been more concerned with equality of opportunity than with equality of goods. This is a measure of social mobility. The Social Mobility Commission in its 2016 report, *State of the Nation 2016: Social Mobility in Great Britain,* came to the following conclusions (these are selectively itemized):

- The early years of a child's life have a lasting impact, but there are stark social class differences in how ready children are for school: in the last decade 500,000 poorer children were not 'school-ready' by age 5.
- What happens in the home is key to child development, but support for parents is weak and provision patchy, even though most want better advice.
- The government's increased investment in the early years is welcome, but there is not enough high-quality provision: poorer children, who stand to gain most from high-quality childcare, are least likely to receive it.
- The cost of childcare for a family with two young children is more than the average mortgage: struggling families are priced out of the best provision and new childcare reforms could make this worse, not better.
- Despite a welcome focus on improving attainment in schools, the link between social demography and educational destiny has not been broken: over the last five years 1.2 million 16-year-olds – disproportionately those from low-income homes – have left school without five good GCSEs.

- Just 5 per cent of children eligible for free school meals gain five 'A' grades at GCSE. The income gap is larger than either the ethnicity gap or the gender gap in schools.
- A child living in one of England's most disadvantaged areas is 27 times more likely to go to an inadequate school than a child living in one of the least disadvantaged. Ten local authorities account for one in five of England's children in failing schools. Poor careers advice and work experience mean that even with the same GCSE results, one-third more poorer children drop out of post-16 education than do their better-off classmates.
- Low-income youngsters are one-third more likely to drop out of education at 16 than better-off peers with similar GCSEs, and are 30 per cent less likely to take the 'A' levels needed to study at a top university.
- Poorer students in areas with school sixth forms do better, but in 20 places in the country there is no access to school sixth forms, and in these areas poorer youngsters are 18 per cent less likely to take Level 3 qualifications.
- Funding is being diverted from second-chance education in further education (FE) colleges to apprenticeships, which are often of low quality, in low-skill sectors, and not linked to the country's skill gaps.
- Despite recent progress, for every child who goes to university from a family in the bottom two income quintiles, seven do not.
- Youngsters cannot access higher education (HE) locally in many parts of the country, exacerbating the gap between those parts of England that are pulling ahead and those that are falling behind.
- Millions of hard-working families have experienced a 5 per cent real-terms average fall in wages since 2008 and young workers have seen a 15 per cent decline in hourly pay.
- Only one in ten low-paid workers – who are mainly women – go on to escape low pay, and in 40 local authorities in England a third of all employees are not paid the voluntary Living Wage.
- 700,000 better-paid, intermediate-skilled jobs have disappeared in a decade, and a regional brain drain is occurring, with more graduates moving from areas with few professional jobs to those with more.
- If current trends continue, 9 million low-skilled people could be chasing 4 million jobs, with a shortage of 3 million workers to fill 15 million high-skilled jobs, by 2022.

- Despite efforts in recent years to change the social make-up of the professions, only 4 per cent of doctors, 6 per cent of barristers, and 11 per cent of journalists today are from working-class origins.
- Home ownership rates among under-44s have fallen 17 per cent in the last decade as their housing costs have grown twice as fast as their incomes.
- Nearly 1 million more households with children rent privately than ten years ago, but they face higher housing costs than those who own their own homes.
- The gap between the housing haves and have-nots is accentuating the wealth divide: people who own their homes have an average wealth of £307,000, compared with less than £20,000 for social and private tenant households.
- Government schemes to help people get onto the housing ladder are welcome, but high house prices mean homes are beyond the reach of almost all average earners.

The Commission reported in 2016 that Britain had a deep-seated social mobility problem: the poorest found it hardest to progress, as did families with an annual income of around £22,500. In real terms, earnings were still 5 per cent below their 2008 peak and housing costs were rising faster than earnings. Social mobility is about an individual's ability to progress in life, regardless of their background. The Commission also suggested that the more social mobility there is, the less someone's destination in life depends on their origins. However, what the Social Mobility Commission did not examine was inequality of goods, basic capability equalities, and those relations between inequalities of goods, basic capability equalities, and social mobility.

The third form then that equality can take is basic capability equality (Sen, 1985), that is, capability for life functions. Elementary functions include being in good health, nourished, sheltered, etc. Social functions comprise having self-respect, taking part in the life of the community, and so forth. Capability refers to the real options that someone has in order to pursue the functions they desire. Furthermore, inequalities of classed, gendered, or dis-abled types prevent the realization of human freedom and thus limit a person's ability to function in society.

There are a number of positions that can be taken on the issue of equality with regard to education. The first position is underpinned by a belief that people are unequally talented because of their genetic predispositions. Improving social and educational conditions cannot ameliorate or change this state of affairs. Resources should therefore be targeted at the more talented, because in order for the less talented to be able to enjoy some measure of esteem in society, that society has to be organized in the most efficient way possible. Furthermore, because the most talented are the driving force behind the provision of esteem for the less talented, they should be better rewarded, not least to motivate them to work harder so that the less talented are provided with the means to achieve that measure of self-esteem. The consequences of this viewpoint are the implementation of a differentiated schooling system and the targeting of different teaching programmes for different types of children (i.e. the more talented and the less talented). Since the measure is a genetic one, various safety devices (i.e. later rather than earlier assessment of ability) need to be set in place to ensure that talent is both recognized and rewarded. Furthermore, if it is deemed that recognition by those less talented of their talentless status does not contribute to the maintenance of their self-esteem, then this should be concealed from them. It should be noted here that this attribution is real, since it rests on a perception that human beings have fixed and innate intellectual dispositions.

The second position is underpinned by a similar belief, that is, that people are unequally talented because of their genetic predispositions, but holds that each should nonetheless be educated to their highest possible level. Even if that educational provision is effective, and in theory it is possible to make it so, this will not then lead to an equality of outcome, because that is an impossibility. Furthermore, since we are dealing with two sets of conditions – social influences and educational provisions – in order to maximize the education of talent to its fullest degree, both issues have to be addressed. Because social and genetic influences act to produce an inequality of learning dispositions, unequal provision or at least differentiated provision needs to be provided for children with different levels of talent and more importantly different levels of cultural capital. Meanwhile, social programmes are required to even out the different levels of cultural capital acquired by children outside the school, even though this will have only a limited effect. There are two reasons for this. The first is genetic predisposition (children therefore learn at different rates) and the second is that however successful the ameliorative programmes in society are, they will never produce equality of cultural capital; thus some children's needs will always be different from others.

The third position introduces a new principle, that of merit. People are equally talented and therefore equally capable of benefiting from education, but some make less effort than others, and therefore – abiding by the principle of natural justice – they deserve to be less well rewarded. A distinction needs to be made here between those dispositions that are in the control of the individual and those outside their control. This is a difficult distinction to make. However, advocates of this strategy need to make it because it provides a justification for the unequal distribution of goods. What tends to happen with this position is that an assumption is made that it is possible to distinguish between the two and that schooling is understood as a testing ground for this strategy, so that those who work hard, regardless of the social conditions which structure their learning and their lives outside school, succeed at school and therefore deserve to be better rewarded than those who do not. An essential precondition for the successful implementation of this strategy is a need to adopt programmes that allow the successful flowering of those dispositions such as effort, diligence, hard work and so forth. A meritocracy requires that the means for the effective exercise of these virtues are not constrained by social and educational factors. Furthermore, although it acknowledges that schools have a part to play in this equalizing of life chances, it also understands schooling as a testing bed for these virtues. At this point it is perhaps appropriate to suggest that the second role for educational institutions, that is, their role as providers of opportunities for the exercise of the virtues mentioned above, needs to be equally resourced for all children.

A final position takes a different form. Poverty and other types of social disadvantage may have an effect on dispositions to learn, not just because resources at home are likely to be limited, but also because poverty may lead to the adoption of short-term goals (i.e. acquiring the basic necessities of life), which may act to limit educational aspirations. Again, two consequences follow from this. The first is that educational provision should be both differentiated and unequally resourced in favour of those children who are less advantaged. Second, proponents of this position argue that equality of outcome is theoretically possible and that what prevents this happening is the way society is organized. Institutional reform (with regard to schools, families, communities) is therefore needed.

Social mechanisms

At this point in the argument being made in this book, we need to understand how one can construe the evidence that we use to show how inequalities and equalities play out in modern societies such as the UK. This involves a claim about knowledge. Roy Bhaskar (2011), in his role as a philosopher of knowledge, makes three claims about the world, and thus also about knowledge of it: (1) that there are important differences between the transitive realm of knowing and the intransitive realm of being; (2) that the social world is an open system; and (3) that reality has ontological depth. The first of these, then, is a distinction between the intransitive world of being and the transitive world of knowing, with the consequence that if they are conflated, either upwards, resulting in the epistemic fallacy, or downwards, resulting in the ontic fallacy, some meaning is lost. There are two implications. Social objects, and the relations between them (i.e. networks, confluences, and conjunctions), though real, are constantly changing, and it is therefore the changing object which endures, even if that object has been so utterly transformed that it is barely recognizable in relation to its former self. The second implication is that, in certain circumstances and within certain conditions, social objects from the transitive realm can penetrate the intransitive realm and be objectified.

This also suggests that the transitive and intransitive realms may become disconnected. Bhaskar identifies four reasons for this: (1) there are social objects in the world whether they are known or not; (2) knowledge is fallible because any and every epistemic claim is refutable (both in the sense that errors can be made and subsequently corrected and in the sense that knowledge is essentially corrigible and relative to other circumstances and conditions); (3) there are trans-phenomenalist truths which refer to the empirical world and discount deeper levels of social reality, that is, the work of social mechanisms; and (4) more importantly, there are counter-phenomenalist truths in which those deep structures may actually be in conflict with their appearances.

The second claim he makes is that the social world is an open system. Closed systems are characterized by two conditions: objects operate in consistent ways, and they do not change their essential nature. Neither of these conditions pertains to open systems. In closed systems measured regularities are synonymous with causal mechanisms. Experimentation is therefore unnecessary because experimental characteristics are naturally present. There are two alternatives: artificial closure, and the use of methods and strategies that fit with systemic openness (including, but not limited to, inferential judgements from the analysis of evidence). The first of these alternatives, artificial closure, makes a number of unsubstantiated assumptions: that transferences can be made even if the original knowledge is constructed in artificial conditions; and that this original knowledge is correctly related to the constitution of the object. The second alternative is that we adopt methods and strategies that conform to the principle of systemic openness. This would seem to be the more appropriate option.

The third claim he makes is that social reality has depth. Social objects are the real manifestations of the idealized types used in discourse and are the focus for any enquiry. They are structured in various ways, and because of this, they possess powers (Brown *et al.*, 2002). The power that these structures (or mechanisms) exert can be one of three types. Powers can be possessed, exercised, or actualized. Powers *possessed* are powers that objects have whether they are triggered by the circumstances or not. Their effect may not be evident in any observable phenomena. *Exercised* powers have been triggered and are having an effect in an open system, and as a result they are interacting with other powers of other mechanisms within their sphere of influence. These exercised powers may still not give rise to any observable phenomena as these other powers may be acting against them. Powers that have been *actualized* are generating their effects; within the open system they are working together with other powers, but in this case they have not been suppressed or counteracted. Embodied, institutional, or discursive structures can be possessed and not exercised or actualized, possessed and exercised, or possessed and actualized. As a result, a causal model based on constant conjunctions is rejected and replaced by a generative-productive one, and objects and relations between objects have emergent properties.

However, this is an indirect realist theory and therefore employs processes of modelling and retroduction to provide accounts of the social categories, how they are practised, and the relations between them over time. This means that the evidence we adduce to support the claims we make in this book are traces and footprints, and only these. However, they have the potential to allow us to develop understandings of those ever-changing mechanisms of gender, class, dis-ability, intelligence, race, and sexuality that constitute our lives. For example, ethnicity is a singularly ill-defined concept. In reality, it is a proxy measure for some notion of race, and includes a narrative (although this is not made explicit) about culture and lifestyle. This narrative may not be relevant to all those who are broadly grouped under some ethnic category or another. Throughout this book, then, we are concerned to try to provide accounts of social mechanisms as they relate to the social categories of gender, class, race, dis-ability, intelligence, and sexuality. In the first instance, we need to examine the role and influence of private and independent schools within the education system, focusing in particular on the social category of class.

Chapter 2

Private education

In this chapter we focus on private and independent forms of education in England. We attempt to understand how they work and their influence on the body politic in relation to the three types of inequality that we identified in Chapter 1: inequalities of goods, inequalities of opportunities to acquire these goods, and inequalities in life conditions. To this end, we need to understand in the first place how schools were first set up in England. The earliest schools here consisted of two types of institutions: grammar schools, to teach Latin to English priests, and song schools, many of which were later transformed into choir schools. In these song schools choristers had certain prescribed duties, such as singing at important Christian festivals. They offered a fairly rigid Latinate curriculum. For centuries, girls were excluded from these song schools, and the aesthetic norm for spiritual singing became the unbroken voice of the boy soprano, supplemented by the male tenor, baritone, and bass voices. These schools then date from the arrival of St Augustine around the end of the sixth century, and it is thought likely that the first grammar schools were established at the same time, with these coming under the authority of the church and being attached to a cathedral.

The grammar schools were different in function from the song schools (Leach, 1915), with the latter being almost exclusively concerned with performances of Christian rituals in the cathedrals and the former more concerned to provide a general education for the professions, as well as for members of the clergy. St Augustine's idea of a curriculum, being derived as it was from the Roman and Hellenistic schools of rhetoric (this word having a distinctive classical meaning and being different from its contemporary common usage), comprised the study of grammar, rhetoric, logic, arithmetic, geometry, music, and astronomy, with these considered to be a preparation for the professions of theology, law, and medicine. In practice these early grammar schools focused on Latin grammar and literature, as they saw their primary function as being to prepare initiates for the priesthood.

Though the church had almost complete control over the education system, such as it was at this time, at the end of the medieval period its authority was contested. The first challenge came in the form of secularization processes and the development of academic specializations such as philosophy, medicine, and law. Charles Taylor (2007) identifies three types of secularism. The first of these is what he calls 'secularity in terms of public spaces' (educational, political, cultural, professional, recreational, etc.), with the understanding that these have now been emptied of references specifically to God or even to some ultimate reality, in other words, some notion of a metaphysical being. The second of these senses of secularity is a falling away of religious belief and observances, so that, for example, fewer people go to church on Sundays. And the third sense that Charles Taylor gives to this notion of secularity is one in which the idea of God or some ultimate reality is challenged at every moment of life and understood as an alternative choice among many others; where the authority of God (and the church) has been superseded by other forms of authority. These early forms of secularity had only a limited influence, as the country was effectively Christian at this time. The second major challenge was the establishment of a university system that was not governed by the church, though its curriculum and many of its observances could still be regarded as religious.

And thirdly, by the end of the fifteenth century the networks of grammar and song schools were joined by newly created independent schools, that is, those independent of the church and the state. These schools were founded for the children of the wealthy elites, though many of them offered scholarships to 'poor and needy scholars, of good character and well-conditioned, of gentlemanly habits, able for school, completely learned in reading, plain-song and old Donatus (Latin Grammar)' (unknown source in Williams, 1961: 132). They developed into what are now known as the public schools, though this term is entirely inappropriate in its modern manifestation, as they are fee-paying, independent of the state, and registered as charities in order to be exempt from paying various types of taxation (18 in total). Two of these independent schools were Winchester and Eton.

During the English Reformation, the grammar school remained central to the system; however, a significant change occurred to the ownership of these institutions, with a typical medieval grammar school being the preserve of the church and the new grammar school being mostly a private foundation. Their curriculum was generally what has come to be known as classical, in that the students read Cato and Aesop, practised Latin letters, wrote Latin verses, translated poets and historians from Latin to English and vice versa, and made 'varyings', which meant that they turned sentences of Latin from their oratio obliqua form to the oratio directa form, and from one tense and mood to another. Greek, and sometimes Hebrew, was added to the curriculum so that pupils could read the scriptures in their original form. However, little of the learning generated by the Renaissance penetrated the very conservative classical curriculum of this time.

In the seventeenth century criticisms were made, generally by the economically wealthy, of the limited curriculum of the grammar schools, that it was too academically orientated. Two other types of schooling were introduced to satisfy the needs of this class: craft and trade apprenticeships, and a form of chivalry training. The existence and indeed demand for these forms of training points to the way in which educational provision in England has always been a response to the socially stratified nature of society. The labouring poor were at this time largely ignored. Education was organized in relation to an impermeable structure of inherited status. During much of the eighteenth century, there were three types of grammar schools: nine public schools, seven of which were exclusively boarding institutions, whose clientele were mostly from the aristocracy and squirearchy; a number of endowed grammar schools, locally based with few working-class pupils; and in addition a large number of city-based grammar schools serving the families of merchants and tradesmen. This last type of grammar school was beginning to widen its curriculum from the traditional Latinate form to a form that embraced new discoveries in science, technology, and mathematics.

In addition, at this time new forms of charity and parish schools were being introduced for all types of children; these, however, provoked controversy, with some arguing that charity schools would make the working poor discontented and potentially revolutionary. Others argued that the state had a moral responsibility towards the mass of children, both urban and rural, and that education would serve to tame their base instincts – instincts that were not held, it was presumed, by members of the higher classes. Divisions of a social nature were fundamentally in evidence in relation to the different categories of schools for different types of children. It was the rapid industrialization of Britain in the eighteenth and early nineteenth centuries that provoked the state into providing a proper and universal education system.

This transformation also contributed to changes to the curriculum of the private and endowed schools. In Rugby School the curriculum underwent a transformation. Though the purpose was still the education of Christian gentlemen, and the classics still formed the foundations of the curriculum, French, mathematics, English, German, ancient history, and modern European history were also taught (see Peel, 2015). By the 1840s, there were about 700 private grammar schools and more than 2,000 endowed schools. Changes in structure and curriculum were rapidly taking place, spurred on by various external examination bodies, such as the London Matriculation Examination Board, the Oxford Local Examinations Board, and others. Girls' education at this time was limited and poorly funded. It included boarding provision, and a distinctive curriculum for preparing girls for their feminine and gendered lives. At a typical girls' school in around 1850, for example, the girls recited French, German, and Italian verbs, read selected texts in these languages and of course English, practised music, dancing, and calisthenics (for strengthening and beautifying purposes), and were instructed in the Christian religion (Ghosh and Goldman, 2006). The main aim was social presentation, which for these girls was rigidly prescribed.

England's education system was being formed along clearly delineated class and gendered lines; and this can be seen most clearly in three important reports: the 1864 Clarendon Report (Clarendon Commission, 2004), which focused on the public schools, and which led to the 1868 Public Schools Act; the Taunton Commission (1868), followed by the 1869 Endowed Schools Act, focused on the needs and requirements of the burgeoning middle classes; and the Newcastle Report (Education Commission, 1861), followed by the 1870 Elementary Education Act, focused on the education of the working classes. The Clarendon Report made recommendations for the governance and curriculum of the nine public schools of the day, namely Eton, Winchester, Westminster, Charterhouse, St Paul's, Merchant Taylors', Harrow, Rugby, and Shrewsbury. These were formally now referred to as public schools and were to be joined at a later point by a great many others (all nominally and actually independent of the state), though within the independent sector distinctions were made between these old and well-established public schools and the rest, which were considered to be inferior. The Commission recommended that their curriculum should consist of classics, mathematics, a modern language, two natural sciences, history, geography, drawing, and music. The Clarendon proposals were incorporated into the Public Schools Act of 1868, which provided for new governing bodies for these schools and empowered the new governors to make their own decisions about admissions, boarding provision, religious observance, term dates, sanitation, new curricula, employment of staff, and the powers of the *headmaster*. (Interestingly, this became the preferred title for the person responsible for the school as a whole, whereas in much of the state sector, the term *head teacher* came to be considered the norm.) The Taunton Commission of 1868 rationalized the endowed sector, recommended that a national system of secondary education should be set up, and urged the government to fund three grades of school. The first-grade schools would provide their pupils with a liberal education, including Latin and Greek, to prepare upper-class and middle-class boys for the universities and the older professions, such as the law and the clergy. The second-grade schools would prepare boys from middle-class homes for the civil service (and especially to administer and direct the affairs of the British Empire), for ranks in the British Army, and for the newer professions, such as in construction, engineering, teaching, and medicine. The third recommended grade of schools was designed to cater for boys from lower-middle-class families, whose destinations were likely to be as farmers, tradesmen, and artisans. Movement between these schools would be limited. Many of the recommendations of the Taunton Commission were incorporated into provisions made in the Endowed Schools Act of 1869.

Raymond Williams (1961) suggested that the debate about education in Victorian and Edwardian times had three strands, represented in three types of educator: the public educators, the industrial trainers, and the old humanists. The old humanists supported a notion of liberal education but feared that it would be vulgarized if it was offered to the working classes, the mass of the population. They also argued, against the industrial trainers, that liberal forms of education would be 'destroyed by being turned into a system of specialized and technical training' (Williams 1961: 142), a debate which points to the contentious vocational/academic divide that surfaced in the twentieth century. Meanwhile, the public educators disagreed with the industrial trainers in that they understood education as being wider than a narrow system of pre-industrial instruction. Williams argued that the influence of these three groups – the public educators, industrial trainers, and old humanists – continued to be felt well into the twentieth century. Class thinking dominated these debates, with arguments being made for separate schools for different classes of children, as education was understood in terms of training for a particular role in life out of which it would be extremely difficult to move. This could be seen most clearly in the different types of curricula offered to the different social classes in the different schools, including those we now consider to belong to the private sector.

In the modern era, despite threats to reform such schools' charitable status, the independent sector has continued to thrive. There are now some 2,500 independent schools in the UK, educating around 615,000 children – some 7 per cent of all British children and 18 per cent of pupils over the age of 16. They are united by their independence from the state in terms of finance and governance, but in reality are very diverse. The sector includes day and boarding schools, single-sex and co-educational institutions, highly selective and all-ability schools, Anglican foundational schools but also some Roman

Catholic, Methodist, Quaker, Jewish, and Muslim institutions. Throughout the nineteenth and early twentieth centuries, these independent schools, and especially the boarding schools, were renowned for their distinctive (and in the eyes of many, arcane) forms of dress, rituals that clearly served no functional purpose, spartan living conditions, preservation of a classical education (and in particular a Latinate one), devotion to certain types of games (rugby and not football, since the latter was considered to be the preserve of the working classes), rigidly defined hierarchies, promotion of a Christian religious form of worship, and a chivalric code of behaviour, understood as both service to the society and support for a rigid class-based hierarchy.

Various attempts were made to change the social class basis of these institutions in the twentieth century, but with little success. The Fleming Committee, convened in 1942, tried to broaden their social class composition by requiring that 25 per cent of their pupil intake comprise state primary school pupils; this was, however, never accepted by the schools themselves. Indeed, further moves initiated by the Labour government of 1974 meant that the sector actually expanded, absorbing and integrating 119 (out of 174) of the direct-grant grammar schools, with only 55 schools of this type accepting control by local education authorities (LEAs). In 1979, a new Conservative government legislated for the assisted places scheme, whereby provision was made and paid for by the government for free or subsidized places for able children whose parents couldn't afford the fees. By 1997 some 75,000 pupils were the recipients of these grants, at a cost to the Exchequer of over £800 million. However, what was becoming obvious was that those taking up places on the assisted places scheme were rarely from working-class or poor backgrounds (the calculation was that only 10 per cent of recipients came from genuinely working-class backgrounds), and in addition, the means-tested selection processes for determining eligibility were based on income and not capital assets, and thus were open to abuse and falsification. The scheme was abolished in 1997 by the then Labour government.

During the various Labour governments between 1997 and 2010, there were calls for the abolition of charitable status for these independent schools. A review of charity law after the 2001 general election, which the Labour party won convincingly, argued that private and independent schools were businesses and not charities, and thus not deserving of charitable status and the consequent tax relief that this entailed. A parliamentary bill to abolish their charitable status was published in draft form in 2004, and this required the retention of charitable status to be dependent on a public benefit test, though what this actually meant in practice was not clear. The Bill ran out of time before the 2005 election but was reintroduced after the successful re-election of a Labour government, and was granted royal assent as an Act in November 2006. The task of enforcing this Act fell to the Charity Commission. Under the Act's provision, in order to retain charitable status independent schools had to show a commitment to working with local LEA schools and offer more free school places to children from low-income backgrounds. The Independent Schools Council warned at this time that in order to pay for both of these, fees would have to be raised, and that this would put in jeopardy many of the poorer schools in the independent sector – in effect making the sector more exclusive. Granted a judicial review in 2010, the Independent Schools Council argued at the Charity Tribunal that too much emphasis had been placed on bursaries for poor children. The Tribunal upheld this complaint and further ruled that some parts of the Charity Commission's guidance in relation to the new law should be revised. They also ruled that it was the duty of the governors and trustees of these schools to decide how best they could meet their obligations under the Act, and especially as these obligations related to matters which were external to the general day-to-day running of the school. The Coalition government and the subsequent Conservative government took no further action to support the central purpose and function of the Act; to this day the settlement by the Charity Commission is at odds with the clear intentions of the Act.

In the earliest days of the formation of the private sector, single-sex education was considered the norm. It was only later that many of these same-sex institutions allowed girls to join their sixth forms and subsequently to become fully co-educational; indeed, the arguments for same-sex education in both the private and state sectors are still being made. These arguments have a number of different strands. Some argue that girls and boys have different learning needs and that in single-sex schools teachers are able to employ gender-specific pedagogies. This argument is supported by the school effectiveness movement, which advocates examination results as its distinctive and exclusive criterion of excellence. For example, the claim is made that girls prefer and work best in collaborative and discussion-based learning environments, which are not dominated, as is the case in co-educational schools, by boys. This argument extends to the idea that single-sex schools help to challenge gender stereotypes and broaden the educational aspirations of both sexes. For example, proponents of this view argue, in single-sex schools 'traditional male' subjects such as science, mathematics, and engineering, and 'traditional female' subjects such as the arts and languages, can be taken up with enthusiasm by either boys or girls. On the other hand, single-sex education is considered by some to stand against the idea that schools should socialize children for life after school, and that sex segregation may act as an impediment to this. Indeed, independent education, with its historical emphasis on same-sex education, has been accused of forming men and women with particular types of subjectivities and particular types of sexualities.

The Clarendon Report of 1864 crystallized the role of the private and independent schools as the 'chief nurseries of our statesmen'. Preparation for the exercise of power in society required the production of a particular type of masculinity. It was held that this could be achieved only through rigorous selection processes based on social class, followed by a prolonged socialization through harsh processes of psychic hardening in a competitive hierarchy in which evolutionary mechanisms such as the survival of the fittest were allowed to play out. Gender roles were conceived of in binary terms. Femininity was understood as being about subordination and weakness, the opposite of the drive to power, and masculinity the converse. Girls were therefore excluded from these bastions of male hegemony. The association of power with a uni-dimensional understanding of gender and social class, as forces which are mutually reinforcing and reproductive, refers here to masculine processes of the suppression of emotion. It refers too to the preparation, through academic competition, to be admitted to the elite universities, and to be initiated into leadership positions in business, the professions, and public life. In addition, particular types of sexuality were being formed based on a muscular Christianity of domination and suppression, especially in the boarding schools.

Curriculum ideologies

The private or independent sector in England is diverse, with four taxonomic sets of ideas dominating what is on offer. The first of these is humanism. This corresponds with, though it is not identical to, Williams's (1961) categorization of old humanism. Its advocates see themselves as guardians of a cultural heritage. They are elitist only in so far as practical, and not ideological, constraints restrict access to these forms of knowledge. Conservative restorationists or cultural transmitters argue that the curriculum should be anchored in the past, and they emphasize canons of influential texts, formal and didactic modes of pedagogy, the inculcation of values rooted in stability and hierarchy, strong insulations between disciplinary and everyday knowledge, strong forms of classification between different aspects of knowledge, and indeed in some cases a belief that curriculum knowledge is either intrinsically justified or even transcendental. Breadth, balance, and depth of curriculum provision are considered to be important curriculum criteria, with the curriculum being argued for here non-vocational in nature.

A second group of schools is driven by a sense of elitism. A principal concern is to ensure the maximum penetration of an elite into the power structures of society. Though they advocate policies designed to maximize examination results and to attract large numbers of students into their sixth forms, the intention above all is to maintain and increase the numbers of their pupils who go to university, and in particular to Oxford and Cambridge. Consequently, the narrow recruitment base they serve is sustained in power regardless of the levels of educational expertise of their pupils. Academic knowledge is seen as a desirable goal, whereas the acquiring of practical skills is seen as less important.

A third category is pastoralism. This focuses on the specific concerns of small numbers of students whose needs are not being met in the state system. The focus is on the social needs of their clientele (both parents and students), and academic success is not considered to be a priority. The curriculum is geared in part to the social and pastoral needs of the pupils. This may involve the adoption of a vocational curriculum, or at least vocational elements may feature in what is still likely to be an academic curriculum.

A fourth category is accountability. The major concern of these schools is to satisfy the needs and demands of their clientele, both students and parents. Choice of subjects, range of options, types of syllabuses, and other related curriculum matters have to satisfy the needs and aspirations of parents. Education and accreditation are understood as commodities to be exchanged for money in the marketplace. The consumer has to be seen to be getting full value for their investment. The emphasis is therefore on the maximization of examination results and the acquiring of cultural capital. Access to sixth forms and universities is considered to be a central goal, although many parents' aspirations may be satisfied at a lower level.

Bourdieu's (1986 and, with Passeron, 1977) notions of material capital, cultural capital, and social capital may be helpful in explaining education's role in creating and reproducing social divisions and economic inequalities, and in particular, the type of influence exerted by the private or independent sector. It is likely that the accumulation of each kind of capital works in different ways; it is also probable that the relationships between them are different. At the end of his seminal essay on forms of social capital, Bourdieu (1986) attempts some broad approximations of the convertibility of one kind of capital to another. He introduces a notion of disguises (and guises) in the mobilization of cultural and especially social capital. The principal idea that he is developing is that in the relationship between social and cultural capital on the one hand and material capital on the other, disguise is fundamental, so that the reproduction of advantages and disadvantages in society operates below the surface of everyday life. Bourdieu suggests that cultural capital, formed and nurtured in private schools, overrides any levelling tendencies that public education systems may have, because of the way the habitus takes years, if not generations, to accumulate and then dissolve. This is not immediately evident and educational policies and practices are not able to eradicate it overnight.

Power and influence: The independent sector

The number of pupils in the independent sector has shown a steady but unremarkable increase since 1974, with a small spike being recorded at the turn of the century (see Tables 2.1, 2.2, 2.3, and 2.4). There is a small but positive correlation between national economic prosperity and numbers of pupils attending schools in the independent sector. The class, ethnic, and gender composition of the student body in the independent sector has changed since 1951, with an increase at secondary level (and to a lesser extent at primary level) in numbers of pupils from abroad, in attendance at single-sex girls' schools, in co-educational schooling, in numbers of day pupils, in ethnic mix (though this is still limited), and in the number of pupils from precariat, traditional working-class, emergent service working-class, technical middle-class, and new affluent working-class families. These trends have been exaggerated by political initiatives, such as the assisted places scheme.

Table 2.1: Full-time pupils in independent schools, 1974–2016

Census year	Numbers of full-time pupils	% of total school population
1974	310,975	6.0
1982	404,542	6.4
1990	474,203	7.2
2000	484,052	7.3
2009	514,531	7.5
2011	506,500	7.2
2016	518,432	7.1

Source: Independent Schools Association, 2016: 8.

Table 2.2: Types of school in the independent sector, 2017

Total number of schools	1,301
Junior schools where all pupils are in Year 8 or below	622
Mixed-age schools	439
Senior schools where all pupils are in Year 7 or above	240

Source: Independent Schools Association, 2017: 6.

Table 2.3: Gender and schools in the independent sector, 2017

Total number of schools	1,301
Co-educational schools	1,021
Girls' schools	169
Boys' schools	111

Source: Independent Schools Association, 2017: 6.

Table 2.4: Day/boarding schools in the independent sector, 2017

Total number of schools	1,301
Day schools	823
Day and boarding schools	478

Source: Independent Schools Association, 2017: 6.

Destination data from the independent sector shows a significant number of pupils attending university (see Table 2.5), with a pronounced bias towards Russell Group universities and in particular Oxford and Cambridge. In the 1950s and 1960s various admission mechanisms were in place in these two universities that favoured pupils from private schools, such as the requirement to have passed Latin or Greek 'O' level (classical languages were more likely to be taught in independent schools than state ones), sporting scholarships, and family connections between some of the colleges and the independent schools. The representation of particular types of educational background, and in particular of the elite schools, in influential and important occupations is dependent on three interrelated factors: the proportion of the population receiving a particular form of education; the recruitment and promotion policies and practices within that occupation; and the predisposition of those receiving particular forms of education. All three of these factors combine to allow elites to prosper and limit social mobility. The influence, though declining, of privately educated elites is shown by the types of school attended by those in elite positions – that is, Members of Parliament (see Table 2.6), senior judges, chairs of Commons select committees, permanent secretaries, diplomats, members of the House of Lords, chairs of public bodies, persons featured in the Sunday Times Rich List, important people in the TV, film and music industries, newspaper columnists, members of the Cabinet, chief executive officers at FTSE-listed companies, and university vice-chancellors in 2015 (see Table 2.7). A persistent bias in the system is still evident and, given the way the habitus as we have seen takes years, if not generations, to accumulate and then dissolve (see Bourdieu, 1986), will continue to restrict the life chances of large sections of the population.

Table 2.5: Destinations of 18-year-olds from the independent education sector, 2017

	Senior	Mixed-age	Single-sex boys	Single-sex girls	Co-ed	Schools with boarders	Day schools	Total
% of higher education inc. university and deferred entries	91.3	91.4	93.0	95.6	90.0	90.5	92.6	91.4
% to university and deferred entries	89.9	89.2	92.0	93.8	88.3	88.6	90.9	89.6
% to re-take 'A' levels	1.3	1.2	1.9	0.9	1.2	1.2	1.3	1.3
% to further education and training	1.2	1.4	0.9	0.7	1.4	1.2	1.3	1.3
% to employment	1.6	2.2	1.2	1.0	2.2	2.1	1.7	1.9
% to other (including unknowns)	4.6	3.9	2.9	1.8	5.0	5.0	3.2	4.2
Total number recorded	22,936	21,301	4,353	7,095	32,789	25,875	18,362	44,237

Source: Independent Schools Association, 2017: 38.

Table 2.6: Percentage of MPs educated in independent schools, 1979–2015

| | Year | | | | | | | | |
Party	1979	1983	1987	1992	1997	2001	2005	2010	2015
Conservative	73	70	68	62	66	64	60	54	48
Liberal Democrat	55	52	45	50	41	35	39	40	14
Labour	18	14	14	15	16	17	18	15	17
All main parties	*49*	*51*	*47*	*41*	*30*	*31*	*34*	*37*	*32*

Source: Social Mobility and Child Poverty Commission, 2014.

Table 2.7: Educational backgrounds in influential social groups, 2015

	Attended an independent school (%)	Attended Oxford or Cambridge University (%)
Senior judges	71	75
Commons select committee chairs	57	37
Permanent secretaries	55	57
Diplomats	53	50
Lords	50	38
Public body chairs	45	44
Sunday Times Rich List	44	12
TV, film and music	44	11
Newspaper columnists	43	47
Cabinet	36	59
FTSE-350 CEOs	22	18
University vice-chancellors	20	14

Source: Social Mobility and Child Poverty Commission, 2014.

In the next chapter, we examine social class, gender, and religious influences in the formation of systems for the training and deployment of teachers.

Chapter 3

Teacher training

Policies and practices of teacher training and preparation in the English education system have been formed and reformed in response to gendered, classed, and religious impulses and influences. These practices, initiated by different governments over the last century and a half, reflect movement back and forth between three models of teacher preparation and teaching practices: craft knowledge development, executive technician processes, and professional learning practices. Craft knowledge has the following characteristics. It is rooted in practice and in the routines that shape practice, and this rules out certain types of learning or pedagogic approaches. This means that imitation and scaffolding various attempts to perform the activities are key to the development of this type of knowledge. The teacher or facilitator is the expert practitioner and knowledge is derived from exposure to the performances of the expert. The expert is therefore not primarily a skilled pedagogue but a skilled practitioner. The emphasis is placed on observing and imitating the practice. The justification for this is that the nature of the practice is better understood in these terms; that is, the learning object, becoming and being a good teacher, is a craft activity.

Craft knowledge values situated understanding and downplays the importance of technical know-how and critical reflection. This leaves little room for what might be called research-based knowledge, even if this is understood in a non-technicist way and as having a non-binding quality to it. Though advocates of craft-based knowledge accept that there may be a role for systematic propositional knowledge, this is confined to what is taught, rather than to the processes of teaching and learning that the teacher or student teacher is engaged in. Furthermore, this entails a clear separation between content and process knowledge or between the learning object and the pedagogic process. In addition, this focus on practical judgements as the essence of the teaching activity fails to account for ethical and epistemological elements in the judgements teachers make. These judgements, as a consequence of their lack of reflective critique and adherence to external expert judgement, may be inherently conservative and potentially unreliable, based as they are on observations of existing practice and common popularizations.

The second of our teacher models is the executive technician. This requires the teacher to perform in a particular way: to have, and be able to execute, a repertoire of pre-conceived actions. In this model, teaching is a rule-based activity and learning is understood as the assimilation of these rules and ways of enacting them, without recourse to critical reflection or situated understanding. In the executive technician model the value of research findings is recognized; however, it is not thought appropriate for teachers to interpret those findings for themselves. Educational researchers generate findings, which are then expressed as protocols for action, and the role of the teacher is to implement these protocols in the most efficient way possible given that there are always situational constraints. One consequence of this is that the knowledge which is being transferred tends to lack a sense of change, emergence, immediacy, or relevance. This positions the learning object, these rules and protocols, outside space and time and effectively reifies it. This also applies to the assimilative and performative functions of learning.

These rules, as they have been identified by researchers and practical policy makers, are external to the setting. They are not situation-specific or even sensitive to the particularities of the setting in which they are being applied. Educational research is understood as the making of nomothetic statements about educational activities; educational disputes about how teachers should behave in the classroom are settled by atheoretical and value-free empirical enquiries; and theoretical knowledge of educational matters is thought of as superior to practical knowledge, with the result that practice is understood as the efficient application of theoretical knowledge constructed by professional experts. Learning at pre-service and in-service levels then is reduced to the assimilation of these rules and to ways of following them in concrete situations such as classrooms. A more refined version of the executive technician model is that educational propositional knowledge should not be understood as being applicable in every possible circumstance and as having a certainty of outcome, but that it can act as a guide to practical action. This brings back a measure of interpretative activity into the proceedings.

Both the craft and executive technician models can be contrasted with a professional teacher model. Professional learning emanates and is derived from an understanding of the characteristics and functions of being a classroom teacher in the context of where that teaching takes place. Apart from the content and methodological knowledge that teachers need in order to plan and teach a lesson, they also have to take a variety of other factors into consideration and integrate them in a coherent, efficient, and pedagogically effective way. Among these are the previous knowledge, schooling biographies, and expectations of their students, the individual differences between them (e.g. capabilities, interests, and motivations), the objectives of the programme and the overall institution, as well as their own pedagogical aims, theoretical assumptions, and values. Teachers have to make a considerable number of instantaneous and ad hoc decisions; they need to react to and take the lead in classroom interactions and modify their plans and methodological procedures according to the needs of students at specific points during the lesson. Ideally they should create an atmosphere that encourages learning and communication and make sure that the task difficulty level is neither too high nor too low. In addition to this, institutions as well as classes have their own particular norms and patterns of interaction and communication. Teachers play a key role in mediating between this institutional culture and their students. They usually determine the content of classroom talk, organize the distinct phases of the lesson, determine the behaviour that is expected from students, select who is permitted to respond to a question or contribute to a discussion, decide what kind of answers are regarded as valid, and so forth.

Professional development in this model is therefore a process of reflection in action, with differing degrees of complexity and reflection on action. Teachers have to be encouraged to experiment with and explore new practices, contents, and procedures in their actual workplace contexts, and to think about their relevance, usefulness, and viability. Reflection, however, can be greatly increased through collaborative meaning-making, dialogue, and discussion among practitioners who can share with one another alternative perspectives, ideas, and experiences. The exchanges between teachers from the same or different schools provide a further level of reflexivity to the teacher development programme, namely reflection on reflection, in and on action (cf. Schön, 1983).

A natural history

In the eighteenth century in England, nascent forms of teacher training were being developed, particularly by the Society for Promoting Christian Knowledge (SPCK), founded by members of the Church of England in 1698. The SPCK was involved in setting up charity schools for poor children, with a view to promoting the practices of Christianity and virtuous behaviours (SPCK, 1711). The early leaders of the SPCK understood school teaching as a skilled craft. It was in the nineteenth century that a systematic form of teacher training at an elementary level began to emerge. At the dawn of the nineteenth century, two influential public figures, Andrew Bell (1753–1832) and Joseph Lancaster (1778–1838), played a key role in establishing the

'monitorial system'. The core of the Bell and Lancaster monitorial syst
was to use promising pupils as monitors (helpers) who taught other pupils in
their class under the supervision of schoolmasters, which can be understood
in modern terms as 'peer tutoring'.

Lancaster promoted his ideas on the monitorial system through
his writings: *Improvements in Education, as it respects the Industrious
Classes of the Community* (1803), and *An Account of the Institution for
the education of one thousand poor children, Borough Road, Southwark;
and of the New System of Education on which it is conducted, to which is
prefixed a sketch of the New York Free School* (1807). The first decade of
the nineteenth century saw the implementation of his system, together with
the foundation of the Society for Promoting the Lancasterian System for the
Education of the Poor in 1808, renamed in 1814 as the British and Foreign
School Society. By 1830 there were about 346,000 children receiving an
elementary education in church schools that followed Bell's monitorial
system and were sponsored by the National Society (Barnard, 1961).

The monitorial system is significant in that it shaped the prototype
of teacher training in England. The earliest teacher training establishments
were located in model schools with model classrooms for teaching
practices. In 1808, the first teacher training college in Britain, Borough
Road College, was set up by Lancaster in the central model school of the
British and Foreign School Society; in 1811 Baldwin's Gardens, which was
transferred to Westminster in 1832, was set up by Bell in the central model
school of the National Society. Bell and Lancaster, through their societies,
placed an emphasis on 'model schools', where the monitorial system could
be demonstrated for all to see, and on 'normal schools' for the training
of teachers in the system. This rudimentary system of teacher training
flourished in England and lasted until the late 1830s.

Despite its economy, in the end the monitorial system proved to be
inefficient. Under the system the monitor was required, without sufficient
training for teaching, to perform a mechanical role as a conduit for
knowledge to flow from the head teacher to the other pupils. As a result, the
quality of their teaching was poor. Moreover, as monitors were elementary
pupils, they were too young to be trained as teachers. Consequentially, James
Kay-Shuttleworth, a British politician, devised the pupil-teacher system to
reform the monitorial system (Education Department, 1898). This system
was officially instituted in England and Wales from 1846 onwards.

Under the 1846 regime, pupil-teachers were selected from among the
ranks of promising children at the age of 13 to be apprenticed to the master
or mistress for a term of five years in elementary schools. They were then

examined by the Inspector on a prescribed, graded syllabus at the end of each year. If they performed successfully, the government paid the master or mistress a grant per annum of £5 for one pupil-teacher, £9 for two, £12 for three, and £3 for each additional apprentice. At the end of their apprenticeships, the pupil-teachers could sit for a competitive examination for a Queen's Scholarship, entitling them to a three-year course at a training college. At the end of the course they qualified as certificated teachers.

In 1903, the Board of Education issued a set of pupil-teacher regulations with the intention of securing 'for the pupil-teacher a more complete and continuous education, and to make the period of service in an elementary school a time of probation and training rather than too early practice in teaching' (Board of Education, 1903: 5). As a result of these regulations, the minimum age for pupil-teachers was raised to 16 except in rural areas, the normal period of apprenticeship was reduced to two years, and a minimum of 300 hours of instruction in approved centres or classes of pupil-teachers was made compulsory. These regulations were followed by advice from the Board of Education, which emphasized the need to make the fullest possible use of secondary schools for preliminary training purposes, by drawing candidates for elementary teachers from the pool of secondary school pupils.

Under the 1903 regulations, pupil-teachers from the age of 16 attended their secondary schools on a part-time basis, which led to a neglect of their own work in the secondary schools. In 1907, a new scheme, known as the 'bursar system', was introduced as an alternative to the existing method of pupil-teachership, enabling full-time secondary education to continue until the age of 17 or 18 with the aid of a bursary grant from the government (Board of Education, 1909). Under this scheme, secondary school pupils of 16 and over who wanted to become teachers could remain at school until 17 or 18 as bursars, and then could enter a training college or become student teachers for a year prior to entering college, spending half of their time in elementary schools for actual practice and the other half in secondary schools for the continuation of their studies.

The bursary system was weakened by the enforcement of the 1921 regulations (Board of Education, 1921), whereby the special provisions afforded to the recognition of bursars were terminated and the provision of special assistance for secondary pupils intending to be teachers lay within the discretion of the local education authorities (LEAs). The monitorial and pupil-teacher systems, run as apprenticeships, can be understood as early forms of school-based teacher training, in that monitors and pupil-teachers were trained in the schools in which they were working.

The training of teachers before 1890 was based on the pupil-teacher system in conjunction with training colleges. Two problems, however, emerged from this arrangement. First, the number of places provided by the training colleges was not sufficient, so only half the pupil-teachers who completed their apprenticeships were admitted to the residential training colleges. Another problem was that most training colleges were religious foundations, mainly Church of England, with the exception of a small number of non-denominational colleges. Consequently, little opportunity for college training was given to those pupil-teachers who had served in board schools with non-denominational teaching. By 1890, there were forty-three voluntary residential training colleges in England and Wales, of which only eight were non-denominational.

During the 1880s, the school boards, dissatisfied with these arrangements, attempted to establish their own colleges in conjunction with neighbouring university colleges (which had not been allowed under the 1870 Act) by presenting their schemes to the government. The Cross Commission was appointed in 1886 to 'inquire into the working of the Elementary Education Act, England and Wales' (Education Commission, 1888: i). In 1888, the Commission recommended that day training colleges should be provided in university institutions. In addition, the government altered the definition of a training college in the Elementary School Code of 1890 (Education Department, 1890: 19), and permitted universities and university colleges to establish day training colleges. According to the code, the day college 'must be attached to some university or college of university rank' in order to be recognized, and the authorities of the college must be 'a local committee' (ibid.: 17–21); maintenance grants and tuition grants were authorized, whilst the length of the course, the syllabuses and regulations for the certificate examination, the requirements of a medical certificate of fitness, and a declaration of intention to teach in an elementary school remained unchanged.

Day training colleges operated on a modest scale in their first decade, yet their advent was to be of great importance to the institutional development of teacher education in England. First of all, it was through these training colleges that the profession of teaching entered university life in England and Wales, breaking the monopoly of the old residential training college tradition and leading to a dual system of teacher training. At this time, the involvement of universities in teacher training in association with training colleges was not seen as advantageous by some university staff, largely due to the poor reputation of the residential training colleges and the social origins of their students. Additionally, it was believed that the elementary teachers did not need a university education (Hyams, 1979). Closer links with the universities were not greatly favoured by residential training colleges either, with the feeling that universities were too academic and not sufficiently vocational. But despite these reservations, with the arrival of these colleges universities began to be much more involved in teacher training.

In 1904, a new type of training college, which was to be maintained by LEAs and needed neither to be residential nor connected with a university, was officially recognized under the new regulations (Board of Education, 1904). After this recognition, the LEA-maintained training colleges, called municipal colleges, grew rapidly, encouraged by the provision of a building grant in 1905. Before the outbreak of the Second World War, the number of training colleges established by the LEAs increased to 28, and their most proficient students were encouraged to stay on for a third year.

By the beginning of the 1920s, the syllabus for the two-year course consisted of obligatory professional subjects – the principles and practices of teaching, hygiene, and physical training – and two groups (A and B) of other subjects, both of which were curricularized in ordinary and advanced courses (Board of Education, 1920). Group A comprised English, history, geography, mathematics, elementary science, and Welsh; at the advanced level elementary science was replaced with physics, chemistry, and botany, and French was added. Group B comprised singing and theory of music, drawing, needlework and handwork (for women only, and known as 'housecraft' at the advanced level) and, at the advanced level only, special handwork and gardening. Students intending to teach in elementary schools had to take at least five subjects: English and one other subject from Group A, two from Group B, and a fifth from either group. Students intending to work in post-primary schools were required to take at least four subjects: English and one other subject from Group A, one from Group B, and a fourth from either group.

After the 1902 Education Act the number of secondary schools increased exponentially, and the government was compelled to take action on the training of teachers for these schools. However, it was in 1908 that the government issued its first set of regulations (Board of Education, 1908) relating to teacher training for secondary schools and recognized a limited number of institutions for training students with degrees or equivalent qualifications as secondary teachers. In 1908, university departments of education accounted for half of the ten institutions that first obtained grants. By 1912, twelve institutions received grants from the Board of Education, of which eight were university departments of education and four were training colleges. Before the First World War, there was a paucity of provision for secondary teacher training.

In July 1911, the government made grants available to facilitate professional training in universities, thereby enabling university departments of education (UDEs) to provide four-year courses, of which three years were for degree studies and a fourth year for professional education. The possession of a university degree subsequently became a requirement for attendance at one of these UDEs. Further, grants were provided to students who signed a 'pledge' promising to teach after qualifying. Although some of these two-year elementary courses in the universities survived until 1951, most did not survive the 1920s. The four-year course system became the norm after 1921 in universities.

It was through the McNair Committee that the training of teachers began to be comprehensively addressed by the government. In 1944, three months before the 1944 Education Act received the royal assent, the Committee made historically significant recommendations through its report (McNair, 1944) on aspects of the training of teachers and on reforms to the educational system, such as the raising of the school leaving age, the expansion of nursery education, a reduction in the size of classes, the ranking of all forms of post-primary schooling as secondary, and the introduction of compulsory part-time education beyond the school leaving age.

In 1961, five months after a three-year certificate course was created, the prime minister, Harold Macmillan, appointed a Committee on Higher Education chaired by Professor Lord Robbins, with the terms of reference to review 'the pattern of full-time higher education in Great Britain' (Committee on Higher Education, 1963: 1). In addition, the Committee reviewed the education and training of teachers in training colleges and made a series of recommendations, which included the raising of the average size of training colleges, the introduction of a four-year course leading to a Bachelor of Education (BEd) degree, the change of the title of training colleges to 'colleges of education', having independent governing bodies and earmarked grants, and the establishment of 'schools of education'. Among these recommendations, those concerning the schools of education and the BEd degree are the most significant in respect of the institutional development of teacher education in England.

The report also suggested that 'teaching should become an all-graduate profession' (ibid.: 112). After the publication of the report, there were discussions between universities and colleges about the degree. The BEd course was introduced in 1964; however, at first, over half the universities with institutes of education refused to undertake the responsibility of validating it. It was not until 1968 that 21 universities agreed to award BEd degrees, although only 7 were prepared to offer classified honours degrees. The first BEd degrees were awarded in 1968 by the universities of Keele, Leeds, Reading, Sheffield, and Sussex, and, in the following year, awards were available in all universities. This four-year concurrent BEd course was revised in 1973. By 1972, the number of candidates for a fourth year accounted for only 10 per cent of the cohort of third year students, which was far from the 25 per cent projected by the Robbins Committee, mainly because of 'the relatively high entry qualifications imposed by both universities and colleges' and 'the anomalies in the BEd structure' (Dent, 1977: 145).

The provision of teacher education increased, with five types of teacher training institutions being set up in England and Wales: university departments of education, colleges of education, polytechnic departments of education, art training centres, and colleges of education (technical). The main training courses during the 1960s and 1970s were the three- or four-year courses, BA/BSc courses, PGCE courses, and other specialist courses. The three-year certificate course created in 1960 by lengthening the two-year certificate course was then further supplemented in 1964 by the introduction of the BEd as we have already seen. The three- and four-year courses also included a small number of concurrent BA/BSc courses, which included undergraduate study of education and a specialist subject, or combined studies with a certificate in education.

The change of government in 1970 provided the momentum to reform the teacher education system. The new Conservative secretary of state for education, Margaret Thatcher, wasted little time before appointing a special committee, chaired by Lord James of Rusholme, with comprehensive terms of reference 'to enquire into the present arrangement for the education, training and probation of teachers in England and Wales' (DES, 1972b: iii). The James Committee was asked to begin its work in early 1971 and to report within twelve months. It duly presented its report in December 1971. The James Report was the first report in the post-war era that addressed every aspect of teacher education, and its principal recommendation was the need to understand teacher education as life-long. It divided the education of teachers into three cycles. The first cycle would consist of the personal education of the student, entailing either two years of academic study leading to a Diploma in Higher Education (DipHE), or a three-year degree. The second would consist of pre-service training and induction, which would last two years: the first year would be undertaken in a professional institution and the second in a school as a 'licensed teacher'; successful completion of this cycle would lead to the awarding of registered teacher status and a BA (Ed) degree. The third cycle would consist of in-service education and training over the rest of the registered teacher's career, each teacher being entitled to one term of training on full pay for every seven years they were employed.

In December 1972, the James Report was followed by a white paper outlining the government's response to its recommendations. In the white paper, the Conservative government rejected the proposed second cycle, featuring the BA (Ed) degree, in the face of growing support for 'concurrent courses for those wishing to commit themselves to teaching at an early stage' (DES, 1972a: 21). Instead, the government suggested new three-year courses that would lead to an ordinary BEd degree and qualified status, incorporating provision for a proportion of students on these three-year courses to continue for a fourth year and take a BEd honours degree. The government accepted the recommendation of the introduction of the two-year DipHE, and envisaged that the two-year DipHE might well be incorporated into the new three-year ordinary/four-year honours BEd courses (ibid.: 22). This was a compromise between the concurrent and consecutive structure in that the government 'allowed for 3+1, 2+2 or 4+0 variants (though tending to prefer 2+2), and encouraged the notion of BEd/ DipHE/BA/BSc flexibility' (Alexander *et al.*, 1984: 111). The existing three-year certificate course was also allowed to continue for the time being as there were not, in the short term, enough applicants who could meet the entrance qualification of two or more 'A' levels proposed for both the BEd and DipHE courses (DES, 1972a).

During the 1960s and 1970s, the PGCE course grew steadily from its position as a new and little-taken route. While admissions to BEd courses fell by several thousand during the reorganization period, the PGCE specification broadened its focus to encompass all kinds of school and teaching settings. In 1980, PGCE admissions for the first time outnumbered those to the three-/four-year courses, registering 10,830 entrants compared to its competitors' 7,017. Against this backdrop, another significant policy change was to make university graduation a requirement for all teachers. In 1977, the Labour government intended that 'there should be as soon as possible a graduate entry into the teaching profession' and that 'from 1979 or 1980 the entry to the existing certificate courses should be phased out' (DES, 1977: 26).

At this time, teacher education became more school-based, with the status and autonomy of higher education institutions (HEIs) in the teacher training process being weakened. The intention of the new secretary of state for education, Ken Clarke, to 'see students actually getting into a classroom for much more of the time while they train' (Clarke, 1991), was now being fulfilled. Under Circular 9/92, students were required to spend at least two-thirds of their time in schools, which – instead of HEIs – now had to provide elements of training in subject-specific teaching methodology. Additionally, all schools, both maintained and independent, were entitled to apply to be partners in the educational market of initial teacher training alongside HEIs, taking 'a leading responsibility for training students to teach their specialist subjects, to assess pupils and to manage classes; and for supervising and assessing their competences in these respects' (DfE, 1992: para. 14).

During the late 1980s traditional four-year undergraduate and one-year postgraduate courses were complemented by new routes to qualified teacher status. The four-year BEd courses and BA/BSc with qualified teacher status (QTS) courses were joined by shortened two-year and three-year undergraduate courses. The traditional one-year PGCE courses were complemented by various new routes: a part-time PGCE, a conversion PGCE, and the articled teacher scheme (ATS). In addition, the licensed teacher scheme (LTS) was introduced for non-graduates.

The government at this time was concerned to attract new populations into the teaching profession and they did this through the introduction of a range of new routes into teaching. Many of these new routes were related to shortage subjects. These routes were in line with the government's strategic intentions in that they contributed to marketization in teacher education by enhancing the notion of choice and diversity. They also challenged conventional models of teacher preparation and the autonomy of the HEIs that provided them, encouraging school-based teacher education.

Government strategies were further reflected in the establishment of a new inspection body. The Education (Schools) Act 1992 created a new non-ministerial government department, the Office of Her Majesty's Chief Inspector of Schools, responsible for managing and regulating a national system of school inspection by independent inspectors in England. The new department was named the Office for Standards in Education (Ofsted). It comprised the old HMCI and his or her staff, and began to operate with an aspiration of promoting 'improvement through inspection'. Ofsted eventually took responsibility for inspecting teacher training programmes, an arrangement which continues to this day.

New forms of teacher training

The Conservative government of 1992–7 made two important policy moves, which were enthusiastically endorsed by the New Labour governments that followed. The first was the introduction of school-centred initial teacher training schemes (SCITTs), which also included provision for encouraging consortia of schools to offer postgraduate courses. These consortia were groups of schools that received funding directly from the government, and they were entitled to use the money at their discretion. The scheme enabled the schools to provide initial teacher training courses without links to HEIs.

The second of these policy initiatives was the proposal for the introduction of the graduate teacher programme (GTP). This was designed to offer a high-quality and cost-effective route into the teaching profession for suitable graduates who did not want to follow a traditional pre-service route, but 'would prefer a tailor-made training route coupled with employment as a teacher'. Moreover, it was designed to meet the needs of schools 'who wish to be directly involved in the training of their own teachers' without developing a SCITT scheme (DfEE, 1996: 1).

From the very start of the modernization strategy, the New Labour government of 1997 was involved in reformulating the idea of teacher professionalism to meet the challenges of globalization. In his opening foreword to the white paper *Excellence in Schools*, David Blunkett, the new secretary of state for education, demanded that teaching should be a 'can do' profession. A further step was taken in the green paper published in December 1997. In this paper, the government set out its intention to modernize the teaching force with the development of what was called a 'new professionalism', spelling out the requirements needed by teachers in a modern teaching profession (DfEE, 1998). This 'new professionalism' policy stream can be understood as the final expression of a thirty-year shift from 'individualized professionalism' to new forms of 'managed and networked professionalism', accepting that 'decisions, about what to teach and how to teach and how to assess children, are made at school and national level rather than by individual teachers themselves' (Furlong, 2005: 120). For some, this signalled a move towards a lessening of the teaching profession's status.

British governments have in recent times redefined their role in relation to the professions, and in certain circumstances have channelled their considerable power to favour forms of technical rationality at the expense of specialized forms of knowledge. For example, British governments have reallocated government funds for in-service training from universities (through the higher education funding councils) to quasi-governmental agencies, and placed strict limits on the types of course that can be accredited for professional development. This further blurs the distinction between discretionary and mechanical specialization, where these are understood as work being organized in the first case to enhance and in the second case to limit the degree to which discretion is appropriate if the task is to be performed successfully, and constitutes a move towards deprofessionalization.

As with the preceding Conservative governments, the New Labour government of 1997 wanted to maintain a competitive market in teacher education. Of particular importance in terms of initial teacher training were seven proposals set out by the government: new national tests for all trainee teachers, to guarantee high-level skills in numeracy, literacy, and ICT; new pre-course provision for trainee teachers; a review of the procedures for awarding qualified teacher status (QTS); a network of schools to pioneer innovative practice in school-led teacher training; more flexible courses for initial teacher training; a boost to employment-based routes into teaching; and a new national fast-track scheme to recruit the best graduates and promote outstanding teachers quickly through the tiers of the profession (DfEE, 1998: 43).

The PGCE had by 1980 become the major route into teaching and its position was maintained and strengthened thereafter. The number of BEd completers decreased from 9,350 in 1994 to 5,900 in 2007. In contrast, the number of PGCE completers increased from 16,110 to 21,080 in the same period. Following the pilot period of 1993/4, the number of entrants to SCITT schemes increased steadily with the active support of the Teacher Training Agency (TTA). Initially, SCITT schemes comprised PGCE courses solely for training secondary school teachers; later, courses for training both primary and secondary school teachers were developed.

From a practical perspective it should be noted that, with the introduction of SCITT schemes, schools emerged as new sites of teacher training, competing with conventional providers for teacher education such as the universities. Currently, schools are strongly encouraged to become fully involved in all aspects of initial teacher education (ITE). This involvement can take one of three forms: a partnership with a higher education institution or a university accredited by the Training Development Agency for Schools (TDA); the establishment of a SCITT consortium, in which a group of schools is accredited by the TDA to provide training; or employment of an unqualified member of staff who is trained via an employment-based programme. In fact, schools are key institutional agents in nurturing these new routes into teaching.

What is striking among a number of policy changes to teacher training under the New Labour governments of 1997–2010 is the rapid growth of employment-based routes (EBRs) into teaching. In October 2000, the TTA introduced the 'flexible PGCE' route to qualified teacher status as a series of measures to increase the supply of teachers. Further flexible routes introduced were the 'Fast Track' and 'Teach First' schemes. These two new schemes are different, but both are in line with a standards and accountability strategy in that they are clearly focused on attracting highly able graduates into teaching. Fast Track is an accelerated leadership programme set up in 2000 by the Department for Education and Science. Originally, it aimed to attract and retain a small cohort of very able graduates and career changers by providing a high-status career pathway.

Teach First (TF) is an EBR-designed initiative intended to recruit outstandingly able graduates who commit themselves to teaching for two years in challenging secondary schools. This scheme reflects the government's new partnership strategy, in that its introduction was led by two business membership organizations, London First and Business in the Community. This scheme represents a further shift in responsibility for teacher education since the introduction of SCITT, with businesses actively intervening in initial teacher education. Furthermore, the development of the scheme was inspired by the highly successful US scheme Teach For America (TFA), with which it shares considerable similarities.

The training, recruitment, and retention of teachers since the early formation of teacher training at the beginning of the nineteenth century have always been phenomena infused with gender, social class, and ethnic influences. For example, until the Sex Disqualification Removal Act was passed in 1919, no married woman was allowed to train and work as a teacher. This Act should have meant greater numbers of women entering and remaining in the teaching profession; however, since there were at this time high levels of unemployment, social pressures on women continued to keep many from choosing to become teachers. In addition, the local authorities continued to use 'marriage bars' to prevent women from continuing as teachers after they were married. If a woman married then she had to give up her teaching post, as is so vividly illustrated in D. H. Lawrence's *Women in Love*. Some women continued to teach after marriage by concealing their married status; others opted for very long engagements. Marriage bars were finally abolished in the 1944 Education Act.

Currently, the profession is becoming increasingly feminized, though not at higher levels (such as headship) and less so at secondary levels. It is now supplemented by large numbers of teachers from abroad, many of whom return to their countries of origin after teaching in the system for a short period of time. As the feminization of the teaching profession gathers pace, there are concerted efforts (at both policy-making and policy implementation levels) to turn it from a professional occupation into a craft and executive technician occupation. The ethnic and religious background of student-teachers and teachers under contract continues to exert an influence on the make-up of the profession and the types of training that take place. In the next chapter, we examine gender, ethnic, and social class influences on the formation and development of the public system of education.

Chapter 4

Selection and de-selection

In Chapter 2 we examined the origins of the English education system and the socially differentiated nature of its formation. In this chapter we take up the story of its formation after the Second World War. Even before the end of the Second World War provision was being made for a selective form of state education, as recommended in the influential *Education After the War*, the 'Green Book' (1941), produced by members of the Board of Education. The prime minister at this time, Winston Churchill, made clear that it was important to 'establish a state of society where the advantages and privileges which hitherto have been enjoyed only by the few shall be more widely shared by the men and youth of the nation as a whole'. However, the imperative here and in subsequent Acts of Parliament supported a notion of equality of opportunity rather than of equality of goods.

The proposals set out in the Green Book were that the divisions between elementary and secondary education should be abolished and the system restructured to create three sectors: primary, secondary, and tertiary. Local education authorities (LEAs) would be responsible for the provision of secondary education and would be responsible for such matters as accommodation, buildings, size of classes, etc. The most important recommendation in the Green Book, however, was that secondary education should be free and compulsory.

Many of these suggestions were taken up by government ministers and incorporated into the 1943 white paper, *Educational Reconstruction*, and subsequently the 1944 Education Act. The white paper argued for the principle of a free, common, and universal system of education: 'the nature of a child's education should be based on his [*sic*] capacity and promise and not by the circumstances of his parents' (Board of Education, 1943: 7). No account was taken of the growing influence of the private sector, or of the way in which this entrenched privilege in the hands of the small number of families that could afford the fees. The 1944 Act replaced all previous legislation and is now seen as the fundamental act of legislation in relation to the state education sector in the UK. There were similar Acts for Scotland (1945) and Northern Ireland (1947), with at this time no separate provision for Wales.

The Act's provisions have been extensively discussed elsewhere (such as Chitty, 2004; Chitty and Dunford (eds), 1999). In the first place they provided for a full and centralized arrangement for state education in England and Wales, with the appointment of a minister for education, whose duties were to 'promote the education of the people of England and Wales and the progressive development of institutions devoted to that purpose, and to secure the effective execution by local authorities, under his [*sic*] control and direction, of the national policy for providing a varied and comprehensive educational service in every area' (Section 1(1)). 'Comprehensive' education was here understood in a different way to how it is now understood.

The Act created local education authorities, whose duties were to provide for the spiritual, mental, moral, and physical development of the community by offering primary, secondary, and further education to the children in their area. In particular, reference was made to differentiated forms of schooling for different types of children, so instruction and training were understood as being appropriate to different ages, aptitudes, and abilities (Education Act 1944, Section 8(1)). Here entrenched in an Act of Parliament was a clear understanding of one of the social categories with which we are concerned in this book: intelligence and capability were to be understood as fixed and innate capacities of individual children. In relation to a second catgeory, dis-ability, the Act made it a statutory duty of the local education authorities to make provision for 'pupils who suffer from any disability of mind and body' (Education Act 1944, Section 8(2)).

Section 17 of the Act set out the arrangements for how these schools should be governed. A primary school was to have a body of managers and a secondary school a body of governors. In county schools, voluntary aided schools (remnants from the previous system), and new LEA schools, the curriculum and matters such as the length of the school day were to be under the control of the LEA, though no special provisions were made for what that curriculum would consist of or even for the most appropriate pedagogical approaches that schools should adopt. One of the most contentious provisions in the Act related to religious education. The Act specified, in addition to various opt-out clauses, a compulsory daily act of worship:

> [T]he school day in every county school and in every voluntary school shall begin with collective worship on the part of all pupils in attendance at the school, and the arrangements made therefore shall provide for a single act of worship attended by all such

pupils unless, in the opinion of the local education authority or, in the case of a voluntary school, of the managers or governors thereof, the school premises are such as to make it impracticable to assemble them for that purpose.

(Education Act 1944, Section 25(1))

This provision was to be adhered to only in spirit rather than in practice over the coming years.

Sections 33 and 34 of the Act dealt with children requiring special educational provision. It was left to the minister of education to identify the different categories of pupils who required special educational treatments. Other sections of the Act dealt with compulsory attendance at primary and secondary schools, and with the school leaving age (set at 15 in 1944; Sections 37, 39, and 40); further education (Sections 41–7); provision for medical inspections in schools and colleges (Section 48); provisions for milk, meals, and other refreshment for pupils in attendance at schools and colleges maintained by them (Section 49); boarding accommodation (Section 50); clothing grants (Section 51); recovering the costs of boarding and clothing where parents could afford to pay (Section 52); provision for recreation and social and physical training (Section 53); ensuring the cleanliness of pupils in schools and colleges (Section 54); meeting transport needs (Section 55); 'special arrangements in extraordinary circumstances' for children to be educated 'otherwise than at school' (Section 56); and arrangements for the medical examination of a child considered 'incapable of receiving education at school' (Section 57). Part Three of the Act set out to loosely regulate what are now called independent schools or private schools. However, these provisions had minimal effects on the curriculum or teaching and learning arrangements of these schools. Finally, the Act provided for a number of complicated arrangements relating to the finances, administration, and governance of these schools. It also set out an important principle, which was to have a profound influence on subsequent educational practices in England and Wales. Section 76 stated that '(i)n the exercise and performance of all powers and duties conferred and imposed on them by this Act the Minister and local education authorities shall have regard to the general principle that, so far as is compatible with the provision of efficient instruction and training and the avoidance of unreasonable public expenditure, pupils are to be educated in accordance with the wishes of their parents'. This provision, in the succeeding years, was to take on a different guise from that originally intended in the 1944 Act.

What the Act did not specify, though the myth has grown in the intervening years that it did, was a requirement for selection in the system. Nevertheless the Labour government elected in 1944 enthusiastically promoted a tripartite system of education, consisting of grammar, technical, and secondary modern schools. Pamphlet No. 1 (Ministry of Education, 1945) told the newly created LEAs to think in terms of three types of state schools at secondary level; in a booklet which accompanied the circular, the government explained that the secondary modern schools were designed for working-class children 'whose future employment will not demand any measure of technical skill or knowledge' (Ministry of Education, 1945: 12). The formation of this tripartite system was a common enterprise between different sections of the political classes, and at its time was considered to be relatively uncontroversial. However, to reiterate, the 1944 Act did not include any references to 'a tripartite system', 'selection', 'the eleven plus', 'grammar schools', or 'secondary modern schools'. James Chuter Ede, parliamentary secretary to the Board of Education at this time, wrote:

> I do not know where people get the idea about three types of school, because I have gone through the Bill with a small toothcomb, and I can find only one school for senior pupils – and that is a secondary school. What you like to make of it will depend on the way you serve the precise needs of the individual area in the country.
>
> (*The Times*, 14 April 1944)

Grammar schools

Grammar schools have been an important part of the UK education system since Tudor times. As we have seen grammar schools were incorporated into the state system only after the 1944 Education Act, though even then there was sufficient flexibility within the Act itself for the abolition of selection. The educational psychologist Cyril Burt argued at this time that children had fixed, innate levels of intelligence, which could be precisely measured, though the evidence that he used to make these assertions was subsequently found to be false (see Hearnshaw, 1979). This manifestation of one of the categories – that of intelligence – which had implications for other categories (such as race and gender), seen and understood in terms of fixed boundaries between notions of strong intellectual potential and weak intellectual potential, was instantiated in a number of different ways, so that it came to entail specialization, selection, differentiation, streaming, setting, and much more.

The Education Act of 1902 first provided for the establishment of what became local education authorities, to provide universal elementary education for children up to fourteen years of age. However, this Act also included provision for secondary education for those children who had the potential to benefit from it. These grammar schools, some newly created, some already existing, charged fees, though the 1907 Act required that they provide at least a quarter of their places as free scholarships. In actual terms the number of free scholarships rose from roughly a third to almost a half, although in some important ways the 'scholarship pupil' was clearly marked out from the fee-paying pupil, thus cementing valuations based on economic capital. However, there were substantial geographical differences in provision and admission, and between different social classes, during the period 1910 to 1939. Rates of admission to grammar schools as a function of social class changed during this period, with the largest proportional increases being recorded for children of the professional and managerial classes. The proportion of working-class children increased, as did the overall numbers of children attending grammar schools; however, the proportion of working-class children was still relatively small (see Table 4.1).

Table 4.1: Social class representation in admissions to grammar schools, 1900–39 (selected social classes)

Father's occupation	Grammar school entrants (%)			
	Pre-1910	1910–1919	1920–1929	1930–1939
Professional, managerial	37	47	52	62
Other non-manual	7	13	16	20
Semi-skilled or unskilled	1	4	7	10

Source: Boudon, 1973, reported in Jesson, 2013.

Though the 1944 Act didn't legislate for a selective secondary system, it did open the way for its introduction. This policy was set out in Pamphlet No. 9, *The New Secondary Education,* published by the Ministry of Education (1947). This policy proposed a distinction between specialized schools for academically able children, technical/vocational schools for those with appropriate practical skills, and 'modern schools' for the rest; there was, it was proposed, to be a 'parity of esteem' between the different types of schools. This idea of parity of esteem was to be reiterated time and time again with regard to the boundaries established between different elements of the social categories: academic/vocational, male/female, abled/dis-abled, black/white, heterosexual/homosexual, innate cognitive ability/innate cognitive disability, and socio-economic advantage/socio-economic disadvantage; in practice, though, such parity of esteem rarely actually existed. What this meant was that selection at secondary level became the key feature of the education system in England (and Wales). There was a high degree of political consensus about these arrangements, though at the time arguments were made that the provisions of the 1944 Act simply reinforced existing class bias. In addition and in discursive terms, exclusive selection procedures were now seen as the logical choice for children of aspirational families. In 1944 there were about 1,200 maintained grammar schools; over the next three decades the total rarely exceeded this figure.

These selective arrangements were flawed in a number of ways. Objections could include the disputed provenance of and meaning given to notions of intelligence and how it plays out in relation to potential; the unreliability of the tests that were used for selection; the fact that coaching and training seemed to have an effect on these purportedly innate qualities; the gender bias that seemed to operate in the administration of the system; hidden forms of social class discrimination in the selection processes, including the eleven-plus examination itself; and perhaps more importantly the inability of the system to operate the precept of parity of esteem in society. (Attendance at a secondary modern school quickly came to be seen as an indication of failure, and could have profoundly deleterious effects on the rest of attendees' lives.)

For all these reasons and others, moves were made in the 1950s to replace the selective system with some form of comprehensive system. However, what was clear was that in many people's minds the 'comprehensive' principle stopped at the school level (i.e. with the creation of the comprehensive school). The establishment in most parts of the country of a comprehensive system did not in practice mean that the learning experiences of all children, even within a single school, were of equal worth. Within comprehensive schools there were forms of streaming and setting, differing timetables and curricula, differing allocations of types of teachers, differing resources (including size of classes), and differing classifications that were used to categorize children, both informally and sometimes formally, enshrined in learning arrangements made in schools. Above all, the use of assessment and examination, coupled with a standards and accountability agenda, persuaded schools that their best interests lay with the ascription of different types of children to particular categories and the erection of strong boundaries between these different categories. The establishment of grammar schools, technical secondaries, and secondary moderns was only one way in which selection is manifested; more powerful manifestations lie in the adoption of particular curricular and assessment processes within the schools of a single type.

These institutional inclusive systems were only gradually introduced. Pioneering local education authorities such as Leicestershire abolished the selective system in their county and replaced it with a system in which all state-educated pupils moved at the age of 11 to a local high school. (Around 7 per cent of the population opted out of the state system and enrolled in private schools.) At 14, pupils (with their parents' guidance) were able to choose an academic course of study, which meant transferring to upper schools, which were in fact the old Leicestershire grammar schools. Note here the way category divisions at an institutional level at the age of 14 were still being maintained. Elsewhere at this time many counties in England and Wales, and some parts of inner city authorities, were converting their systems to notionally comprehensive ones.

In 1964, a Labour government was elected in the UK and the new minister for education, Anthony Crosland, published Circular 10/65, 'requesting LEAs to prepare plans for moving to a non-selective education system' (DES, 1965). Subsequently, and in an uneven fashion, the transformation of the tripartite system into a comprehensive system proceeded at pace. Some authorities such as Kent and Lincolnshire held out against being reorganized, so that a rough tally (maintained to this day) of 160 grammar schools remained in operation by the early 1980s (see Table 4.2).

Hardly surprisingly there was a furious counter-attack against the abolition of grammar schools, which continues to this day. One form this opposition took was the publication of a black paper that argued strongly for a return to selective education. Three significant papers were produced at this time: 16/83, *School Standards and Spending: Statistical analysis,* and 13/84, *School Standards and Spending: Statistical analysis – A further appreciation,* both by the Department of Education and Science (DES), and *Standards in English Schools* (Marks *et al.,* 1983) by the National Grammar Schools Association. The first of these strongly argued that any performance gains shown by selective LEAs was directly related to the social class composition of the grammar schools and was not due to the selective process per se. The second of these reports argued that the available data at this time pointed to improved examination results as a consequence of the selective system in general, an effect seen across all parts of the tripartite system. The third report suggested that the real benefit of selective education was that bright children from working-class backgrounds would be advantaged by it, or at least that in terms of social mobility some of the barriers to successfully achieving their potential could, through selective education, be removed.

Table 4.2: Number of maintained grammar schools and pupils, 1947–2016 (England and Wales to 1969, England only thereafter)

Year	Maintained grammar schools	Maintained secondary school pupils taught in grammar schools (%)
1947	1,207	37.8
1952	1,189	28.8
1957	1,206	25.6
1962	1,287	25.0
1967	1,236	24.5
1972	883	17.3
1977	407	6.9
1982	189	3.3
1987	154	3.1
1992	157	3.8
1997	158	4.2
2002	161	4.5
2007	164	4.7
2012	164	5.0
2016	163	5.2

Source: Bolton (2016: 10).

However, the comprehensive movement was sweeping the country, with most local education authorities turning their selective systems into comprehensive ones, and this meant the abolition of grammar schools. The 1976 Education Act (which was ultimately repealed by the new Conservative government of 1979) reaffirmed the principle of comprehensivization in clear terms:

Local Education Authorities shall, in the exercise and performance of their powers and duties relating to secondary education, have regard to the general principle that such education is to be provided only in schools where the arrangements for the admission of pupils are not based (wholly or partly) on selection by reference to ability or aptitude.

(Education Act 1976, Section 1(1))

However, the effect of the Act was diluted by the many conditions written into it; these meant that some of the existing grammar schools were able to survive. Besides, though the principle of comprehensivization had been affirmed at the school level, this didn't mean that it operated at classroom levels. Many of these comprehensive schools operated covert policies that differentiated types of students through streaming and setting practices. These schools were nominally comprehensive, but in practice operated clear policies differentiating students.

These debates continued in one form or another up to the present day, as we can see in remarks from a recent cabinet member, David Willetts:

People genuinely worried about social mobility believe that grammar schools can transform the opportunities of bright children from poor areas. For those children from modest backgrounds who do get to grammar schools the benefits are enormous... But the trouble is that the chances of a child from a poor background getting to a grammar school in those parts of the country where they do survive are shockingly low. We must break free from the belief that academic selection is any longer the way to transform the life chances of bright poor kids... there is overwhelming evidence that such academic selection entrenches advantage, it does not spread it.

(Ford, 2007)

Grammar and secondary modern schools are not spread evenly throughout the country. Although the figures presented in Figure 4.1 are for 1998, little has changed since then. This geographically uneven distribution means that comparisons of pupil populations at schools of these two different types are difficult to make. The following comparisons are based on areas that have both grammar and secondary moderns (many of which are now converting or have converted into academies, meaning that they operate to some extent independently of LEAs). These are proxy comparisons.

Figure 4.1: Grammar school areas and groupings, England, 1998. Authorities where whole districts operate a selective system and children routinely sit grammar school entry examinations are shown filled, while circles indicate isolated grammar schools or clusters of grammar schools, as identified by the *Education (Grammar School Ballots) Regulations 1998, Statutory Instrument 1998 No. 2876*, UK Parliament

Source: Wikipedia (2012).

Although we have to be careful about the conclusions we draw here, we can compare grammar schools, secondary modern schools, and secondary schools of all types in terms of their recruitment of pupils by special educational needs, first language, ethnicity, and eligibility for free school meals (see Table 4.3).

Table 4.3: Pupil characteristics by selected school type, January 2016

	Pupils (%)		
Characteristic	Grammar school	Secondary modern school	All secondary schools
With special educational needs but without statements or EHC plans	4.0	12.0	11.0
With statements of special education needs or EHC plans	0.5	3.0	2.5
First language not English	14.0	13.5	16.0
Non-white	30.0	16.0	24.0
Known to be eligible for free school meals	3.0	12.0	14.0

Note: EHC plans refer to education, health, and care plans. In England in January 2016, pupils in state-funded schools were entitled to receive free school meals if a parent or carer was receiving certain eligible state benefits: income support, income-based jobseeker's allowance, income-related employment and support allowance, support under part four of the immigration and asylum act, the guaranteed element of state pension credit, child tax credit, and working tax credit run-on. Infant pupils (though not represented in this table) are also all entitled to free school meals.

Source: Bolton (2016: 6).

Unsurprisingly these different types of schools in different parts of the country produced differing examination results (see Table 4.4).

Table 4.4: Summary of GCSE achievement by mainstream school type, 2014/15

Type of school	Number of pupils	5+ A*–C grades %	5+ A*–C grades inc. English and Maths %	5+ A*–C GCSE only % (exc. equivalents)	% entered for GCSEs or equivalent	% entered for all components of English Baccalaureate	% passing English Baccalaureate
Comprehensive school	501,242	66.3	56.7	58.3	99.5	38.2	23.1
Grammar school	22,493	99.1	96.7	94.8	100.0	77.3	69.7
Secondary modern school	19,329	60.3	49.7	48.9	99.6	26.9	13.9
All state-funded schools	543,314	67.4	58.1	59.5	99.5	39.4	24.7
Independent school	46,361	67.4	58.1	45.8	98.6	15.0	11.9
All mainstream schools	589,675	67.4	58.1	58.4	99.4	37.5	23.7

Source: DfE (2016a: Table 5b).

The data shows that some ethnic minority groups, such as Indian, Chinese, and pupils of other Asian ethnicity, were over-represented in grammar school intakes in 2016 (Andrews *et al.*, 2016). It also suggests that there were fewer poorer pupils in grammar schools than in other types of maintained schools in England. This can be explained partially by the geographical location of these schools, since they tend to be located in more affluent areas of the country. Pupils in grammar schools, it is claimed, achieve slightly higher GCSE grades than their peers of a similar background who attend non-selective schools. But this grammar school boost disappears if the comparison is limited to grammar school pupils vs those at high-achieving non-selective schools, even though these latter are more socially representative of the population of the country. In *Understanding Grammar Schools* (2016) Education Datalab looked at the background of pupils. They found that at the end of key stage 4 in 2014/15, out of 22,497 pupils in grammar schools 3,000 (13 per cent) had attended independent primary or preparatory schools, whereas 7 per cent were from deprived backgrounds. In the same academic year the proportion of entrants at Year 7 into grammar schools from independent primary or preparatory schools was 11 per cent.

Selective testing

Between the First and Second World Wars more and more boys and girls were being accepted on scholarships into the grammar schools, but fee-paying in these grammar schools continued right up until 1945 (when it was abolished by the 1944 Education Act). There existed a differential scale for paying fees, varying according to a child's parents' income. Some children from very poor families paid nothing at all, and in addition were given free dinners. Other parents who earned more than a subsistence wage had their books paid for by the school, and wealthy parents who chose not to have their child privately educated paid fees in full. The means for selecting children to receive scholarships changed several times during the first half of the twentieth century, but all the methods employed involved some form of examination or test, followed if this proved necessary by an interview with the head teacher.

A typical test set for scholarship places in 1910 consisted of four subjects: arithmetic (see Box 4.1), English grammar, comprehension, and literary expression, the latter consisting of an essay chosen from a list of four titles (see Box 4.2).

BOX 4.1: ARITHMETIC TEST, 1910 (SELECTED EXAMPLES)

1. Multiply six millions five hundred and eighty three thousand and twenty by 6,309 and divide this product by 701 (answer in figures).
2. Add together 75 tons, 3 hundredweight, 10 lbs; 33 tons, 1 hundredweight, 16 lbs; and 125 tons, 2 hundredweight, 3 quarters, 2 lbs and find the value of the whole at 5s. 73 pence per quarter.
3. A cistern containing 60 gallons is one third full; the supply pipe conveys into the cistern 21 gallons a minute and a discharge pipe lets out 1 gallon, 3 quarts a minute. If these two pipes are opened at the same time in what time will the cistern be full?
4. How many yards worth 4s. 23 pence a yard must be given in exchange for 402 yards at 3s. 51 pence a yard?
5. Divide £89 17s 6d by 19.75.

   Source: Gateshead Education Committee, 1910, cited in Meads (1998).

BOX 4.2: ENGLISH GRAMMAR AND COMPOSITION, 1910 (SELECTED EXAMPLES)

1. Parse fully the following sentence: By crossing the river a little farther up, he got safely across.
2. Analyse the following passages:
   (a) Lives of great men all remind us
       We can make our lives sublime.
   (b) Such were the sounds that o'er the crested pride,
       Of the first Edward scattered wild dismay,
       As down the steep of Snowdon's shaggy side
       He wound with toilsome march his long array
3. What is meant by inflection, conjugation, tense, co-ordinated sentence?
4. What is an abstract noun? What abstract nouns are derived from the words: young, child, thrive, hot, free, strong, friend?
5. What two methods are there of comparing English adjectives? Write down the positive degree of: prettier, most, less, worst, first.
6. What are weak verbs? Give the past tense (first person singular only) and the perfect participle of: come, bereave, eat, ride, swim and swing.
7. Point out the effect of the prefix in each of the following words: aboard, avert, antecedent, antiseptic, encourage, inveterate, inaccurate, gainsay, withstand.

8. Write a short essay on one of the following subjects:
   (a) The uses of electricity
   (b) A man is known by his company
   (c) Honesty is the best policy
   (d) The qualities which make a great man
   Source: Gateshead Education Committee, 1910, cited in Meads (1998).

These tests can be compared with a 1933 entrance examination paper in arithmetic, taken at the age of 11 (see Box 4.3).

Box 4.3: Arithmetic entrance paper, 1933

1. A package of money contains 27 half-crowns, 19 florins, 37 shillings, 41 sixpences, and 11 three-penny pieces. How much must be added to make the total sum up to £10 10s. 0d.?

2. The first piece cut from the cloth was one-third of the roll, the second piece cut was one-quarter of what was left. The third piece cut was twice as long as the second and the fourth piece was 2 yards long. There remained a remnant which was three-quarters of a yard. What length of cloth was in the roll before the first piece was cut?

3. Entertainment tax on a six-penny ticket is one penny, on a shilling ticket 2½d., and on a two-shilling ticket 5d. At a concert 280 people paid sixpence, 166 paid one shilling, and 97 paid two shillings. The payments included tax. What was the total amount taken and what percentage of this was paid as tax?

4. A War Savings Certificate costs 16s, and at the end of seven years, with added interest, becomes worth £1. The Post Office Savings Bank allows sixpence a year interest on each £1. What would be the difference at the end of seven years between which £4 would become if: a) Used to buy War Savings Certificates? b) Put in the Post Office Savings Bank?

5. A rectangular piece of wood, 14.5 inches long and 18.4 inches wide, is cut up into three rectangular pieces – one is 10.6 inches x 5.7 inches, the second is 3.9 inches, and the third is 2.7 inches wide. Find the area of each of these three rectangles and the length of the third.

   Source: Staffordshire Education Committee, 1933,
   cited in Meads (1998).

This comparison can be extended to an amalgam of three English papers administered between 1928 and 1932 (see Box 4.4). The paper examined a pupil's skills in English grammar, punctuation, spelling, comprehension of the printed word, antonyms, and synonyms, together with a short essay taken from a variety of set topics.

> **BOX 4.4: ENGLISH EXAMINATIONS, 1928–32: A SELECTION OF QUESTIONS**
>
> Time allowed: 1 hour 30 minutes.
>
> 1. Copy out the following passages, putting in punctuation marks or capital letters as needed:
>
>   the good ship s.s. victoria ploughed its way relentlessly through the waves its captain being determined that the victoria would reach liverpool before the connecting boat train left lime st station on its way to manchester
>
>   tuesday was ians least favourite day my oh my he moaned when will it ever end
>
> 2. Write synonyms for the following words: (a) glad (b) huge (c) foolish (d) error (e) lucky (f) monarch (g) forceful (h) obedient (i) selfish
>
> 3. Write antonyms for the following words: (a) forget (b) hearten (c) obstruct (d) ancient (e) offend (f) villain (g) hesitant (h) constant
>
> 4. Arrange the following words into groups, one headed masculine the other headed feminine: goose, hero, conductor, nurse, negress, tiger, engine driver, sailor, docker, waitress, usherette, cow, sow, priest, abbess, magician, footballer, sentry.
>
> 5. What do we call a group of: cows, lions, monkeys, hounds, flowers, warships.
>
> 6. What is a proper noun? Give five examples of such nouns.
>
> 7. What are the superlative forms of the following adjectives:
>   (a) good (b) large (c) happy (d) proud (e) great (f) fortunate (g) beautiful (h) bad (i) pretty (j) enormous (k) stupid (l) kind.
>
> 8. What are the comparative forms of the following adjectives:
>   (a) spritely (b) choicest (c) wettest (d) hungry (e) loveliest (f) muddy
>
> 9. What is the infinitive of the following verbs:
>   (a) found (b) saw (c) roared (d) was (e) gave (f) made (g) became
>
> 10. Add a suitable adverb to the following verbs:
>   (a) roared (b) jumped (c) ran (d) cried (e) moved (f) laughed (g) smiled
>
> 11. Give the plural form of the following nouns:
>   (a) journey (b) monkey (c) parent (d) army (e) navy (f) calf (g) half
>
> 12. What is an interjectory word? Give five examples.
>
> 13. What is a pronoun? Give three examples of words which could be used as pronouns.

14. What do we call a word which joins parts of sentences together?
15. Read the following passage carefully then answer the questions you find at the end of the passage.

Horatio Viscount Nelson 1758–1805

Horatio Nelson was born at Burnham Thorpe, Norfolk where his father was a rector and he entered the navy in 1770. Whilst serving in the West Indies he married Mrs. Francis Nisbet. He was on almost constant active service in the Mediterranean from 1793 to 1800. As the result of battle wounds he lost the sight of his right eye in 1794 and his right arm in 1797. His share of the Navy's victory off Cape St. Vincent made him a national hero and he was promoted to be Rear Admiral as a result of the victory. In 1798 he virtually destroyed the French at the Battle of the Nile.

   (a) What was Nelson's first name?
   (b) In which county was he born?
   (c) What was his father's profession?
   (d) Which country was the British fleet fighting?
   (e) What does the word 'virtually' mean in the next-to-the-last line?
   (f) Where was he when he married?
   (g) What was the name of Nelson's wife's first husband?
   (h) Was Nelson the sole victor of the Battle of Cape St. Vincent? Which word tells you if this was so or not?
   (i) Which limb did Nelson lose?
   (j) How old was Nelson when he died?

16. Several words are wrongly spelled in this passage. Write the correct spelling of these words.

   There swords were safely sheathed when the captane of the ship came to inspect his victorous crew. Smiles abounded as the grate man past in front of the line of sailors and complemented all on their brave deeds as he went by.

17. Write a short story using one of the following titles
   (a) A night of fear
   (b) My holiday at the seaside
   (c) My best friend
   (d) The day when it all went wrong
   (e) My secret wish

Source: Gateshead Education Committee, 1928–32, cited in Meads (1998).

The issue of curriculum-free tests is very much alive, as the current eleven-plus examination in Kent, one of the remaining areas in the country that has retained selective education, shows (Box 4.5).

BOX 4.5: KENT ELEVEN-PLUS TEST: SPECIMEN QUESTIONS

The tests are multiple choice, with a separate answer sheet. They are marked by an automated marking machine. The first test will be an English and Mathematics paper and will take 1 hour. Each section will involve a 5-minute practice exercise followed by a 25-minute test. The English section will involve a comprehension exercise as well as some additional questions drawn from a set designed to test literacy skills. The second test will be a reasoning paper. It will take about one hour, including the practice sections and questions. It will contain a verbal reasoning section and a non-verbal reasoning section of roughly the same length. The non-verbal reasoning will be split into short sections, administered and timed individually. There will also be a writing exercise, which will not be marked but may be used by a local head teacher panel as part of the head teacher assessment stage of the process. 40 minutes will be allowed for the writing task, including 10 minutes' planning time.

1. Verbal reasoning
In these questions, the same letter must fit into both sets of brackets, to complete the word in front of the brackets and begin the word after the brackets.
i) dis [?] urt ii) muc [?] ole
p   h   e   s   k

The answer is *h*.

2. English
In this question you have to choose the best word, or group of words, to complete the sentence so that it makes sense and is written in correct English. You should choose one of the five answers and mark its letter on the answer sheet below.

The letter was stained and crumpled but in the bright moonlight I could still ... almost every word.
(a) Reed   (b) Wrote   (c) Read   (d) Write   (e) Red

The answer is (c), because *read* is the word that makes the best sense in the sentence as a whole.

Pandas
Read the passage, then answer the question that follows.

The giant panda is a bear native to south central China. It has a black-and-white coat and is easily recognized by the large, distinctive, black patches around its eyes, over the ears, and across its round body. Scientists think that the bold colouring provides effective camouflage for the pandas in their snowy and rocky habitat. The giant panda's thick, woolly coat keeps it warm in the cool forests of its habitat. Pandas can be four to six feet long and male pandas can weigh up to 160 kg, which is about the same as two humans.

Why do scientists think pandas have a black-and-white coat? Pandas have a black-and-white coat ...
(a) to attract other pandas.
(b) to make it easier to spot pandas.
(c) to keep pandas cool in the summer.
(d) so that pandas blend in with their environment.
(e) so that pandas look different from other bears.

The answer is (d).

3. Mathematics
I think of a number. I then double it. Next I subtract 6. The answer is 14.
What was the number I started with?
16   22   4   40   10

The answer is *10*.

Source: Kent County Council, 2017.

All these papers seek to test for some notion of general intelligence; in reality, what they do is make some form of assessment of a narrow range of skills in a time-bound and context-specific environment, with no guarantee that the candidate could perform the same set of skills at different time-points and in different environments. However, since future judgements will be made about jobs, universities, etc., using the same evaluative criteria and technologies, perhaps what this shows is a capacity or otherwise to perform well in certain bounded circumstances. It cannot and does not denote any general intelligence capability.

New forms of selection

Since comprehensivization, successive governments have sought to reintroduce selection or selective processes under different guises. In 1987 the then Conservative government introduced city technology colleges in an attempt to involve private business in state education. In the end only a handful of city technology colleges were ever established, as businesses were not in the end motivated to fund them. The new guise for selection was specialism. John Patten, recently appointed to the Department for Education in 1992, argued that:

> Selection is not, and should not be, a great issue of the 1990s as it was in the 1960s. The S-word for all socialists to come to terms with is, rather, 'specialisation'. The fact that children excel at different things; it is foolish to ignore it and some schools may wish specifically to cater for these differences ....
>
> (Patten, 1992)

A white paper of the same year, endorsed by Patten, argued that 'uniformity in educational provision presupposes that children are all basically the same and that local communities have essentially the same educational needs. The reality is that children have different needs: hence our commitment to diversity in education' (DfEE, 1992: 3–4).

The New Labour government of 1997 produced its own white paper, and in it were clear specifications for specialist schools. In the white paper, the new secretary for state made two key proposals: secondary schools would be encouraged to become 'specialist schools', which would be allowed to select a small proportion of their pupils on the basis of 'perceived aptitudes'; and class sizes for five-, six-, and seven-year-olds would be reduced to 30 pupils or fewer. Funding would be provided to enable LEAs to meet this target. The remainder of the paper set out a host of other measures: at least an hour a day in primary schools would be spent on English and an hour on mathematics, reflecting a National Literacy Strategy that was introduced in September 1998 and a National Numeracy Strategy that followed in September 1999. Schools were to have targets for raising standards. School performance tables would show the rate of progress pupils had made, as well as their absolute levels of achievement. Achievements of ethnic minority pupils were to be raised and racial harmony promoted, while special educational needs were to be an integral part of the wider programme for raising standards. Better support was to be offered in schools for pupils with behaviour problems. Education Action Zones would be set up to provide targeted support in deprived areas. Secondary schools were to use innovative approaches and mixed-ability teaching where it proved to be effective, but setting was recommended, particularly for science, mathematics, and languages – and schools were to tell parents about their pupil grouping policies. There would be more family learning schemes where parents and their children could learn together: family literacy courses started in more than 60 LEAs in September 1997. In addition, there would be national guidelines for homework and after-school homework centres. There would be better support for newly qualified teachers and better training for existing teachers, focusing particularly on literacy, numeracy, and IT. Lastly, there would be a national training scheme for existing and new head teachers.

The white paper's proposals were implemented in the School Standards and Framework Act (24 July 1998), which allowed maintained secondary schools to 'make provision for the selection of pupils for admission to the school by reference to their aptitude for one or more prescribed subjects' (Section 102). It also defined the responsibilities of LEAs and gave the secretary of state powers to ensure that they fulfilled them. Both LEAs and the secretary of state were empowered to intervene in schools judged to be 'failing' by Ofsted: such schools would be given two years to improve, and if they failed they would be closed or have radical management changes imposed on them. The Act also set out a new framework for schools (to be implemented from 2000), with community schools replacing county schools and foundation schools replacing grant-maintained schools. Voluntary schools (most of which were church schools) were unaffected. In January 2000 the New Labour government announced that many comprehensive schools would be turned into specialist colleges over a three-year period. These specialist colleges were the forerunners of the academies soon to become widespread in the school system: academies operate with some measure of control independent of the LEA over their curriculum, budget, and staffing. Under these initial Labour proposals, they could achieve specialist status only by being sponsored by local businesses to the tune of £50,000. The Department for Education and Skills would then give them a £100,000 capital grant and guarantee £120 extra per pupil per year for at least four years. In addition they would be allowed to select up to 10 per cent of their intake in terms of aptitude, so pupils that showed promise in modern languages would be prioritized in the admissions policies of modern language academies, and likewise pupils who showed promise in science would be prioritized in the admissions policies of science academies.

The problem with selection by aptitude was that in effect it became selection by general ability, proving very similar to the practice of selection by intelligence under the old tripartite system. The Education Select Committee in 2003 produced a report suggesting just this: '(w)e are not satisfied that any meaningful distinction between aptitude and ability has been made and we found no justification for any reliance on the distinction between them' (House of Commons, 2003). Though the rule was that these specialist academies could select only 10 per cent of their intake and that the rest of their pupils had to be representative of the local population as a whole, some of the academies found ways to circumvent this rule. They selected in terms of bands or levels of academic ability, but then chose pupils from the top of each of these bands. The academies also operated selective policies through exclusions, using this form of de-selection to choose the pupils they wanted. The academies were exempt from financial penalties for exclusions in a way that LEA schools were not. In 2009 the Labour government then announced that they would extend the secondary academies programme to primary schools.

Another form of covert selection is practised by the faith school sector. (Today the faith sector, reflecting the diversity of the schools sector as a whole, comprises a mixture of community, foundation, voluntary aided, voluntary controlled, sponsor-led academies, academy converters, free schools, university training schools, and studio schools; see Table 4.5.) Faith schools already make up one-third of the state sector by school numbers; in the main Church of England or Roman Catholic, but their numbers include Jewish, Muslim, Sikh, Seventh Day Adventist, and Greek Orthodox Schools (see Table 4.6). There was a concern that these faith schools discriminated against children of other faiths, and yet this seemed to be their function. In September 2008 it became legal for maintained schools to select teachers and teaching assistants on the grounds of religious observance. More serious still was the attempt to mask the selection of pupils by intelligence by pretending that selection was only as a result of religious observance. Allan (2008), for example, found evidence to suggest that faith schools were selecting pupils by social class. In deprived urban areas faith schools admitted 10 per cent fewer children from poor families than was representative of the local area. Allan also suggested that faith schools admitted over 50 per cent more pupils from what they considered to be the top quarter of the ability range. Faith schools are required to follow the national curriculum, but they are allowed to choose what they teach in religious studies. They have different admissions criteria and staffing policies than state schools. However, faith academies do not have to teach the national curriculum and have their own admissions processes.

Table 4.5: Mainstream state-funded faith schools in England by type, 2016

	Primary faith schools	Primary non-faith schools	Primary faith schools (%)	Secondary faith schools	Secondary non-faith schools	Secondary faith schools (%)
Community	0	7,267	0	0	515	0
Foundation	25	617	4	3	244	1
Voluntary aided	2,994	33	99	249	18	93
Voluntary controlled	2,014	34	98	22	20	52
Academy: sponsor-led	216	878	20	98	523	16
Academy: converter	893	1,678	35	242	1,229	16
Free school, university training school, or studio school	38	98	28	25	192	12
Total	6,180	10,605	37	639	2,741	19

Source: Long and Bolton (2017: 16).

The Conservative government elected in 2015 sought to further undermine the policy of comprehensivization, and replace it with forms of selection by ability, aptitude, or intelligence. In 2015 they published a consultative document (Department of Education, 2015), an updated version of one published at the beginning of the Liberal Democrat–Conservative Coalition government of 2010–2015, which stated its intention clearly: 'to create a more autonomous and diverse school system that offers parents choice and concentrates on improving standards'. The document listed a number of policies that it would continue to implement, such as encouraging primary and secondary schools to become academies; encouraging strong academies to work with weaker ones; encouraging teachers, charities, parents, and others to establish new free schools, maintain existing ones, and set up new studio schools and university technical colleges.

Table 4.6: Religious character of schools, 2016

	Primary schools: number	Primary schools: %	Primary pupils: thousands	Primary pupils: %	Secondary schools: number	Secondary schools: %	Secondary pupils: thousands	Secondary pupils: %	Total schools: number	Total schools: %	Total pupils: thousands	Total pupils: %
No religious character	10,609	63.3	3,107	71.9	2,743	82.6	2,482	79.3	13,352	66.5	5,619	75.5
Church of England	4,378	26.1	815	18.9	209	6.3	191	6.1	4,587	22.8	1,006	13.5
Roman Catholic	1,642	9.8	416	9.6	315	9.5	295	9.4	1,957	9.7	711	9.6
Methodist	25	0.1	4	0.1	0	0.0	0	0.0	25	0.1	4	0.1
Other Christian	69	0.4	13	0.3	79	2.4	76	2.4	148	0.7	89	1.2
Jewish	36	0.2	11	0.3	12	0.4	8	0.3	48	0.2	19	0.3
Muslim	13	0.1	4	0.1	14	0.4	5	0.2	27	0.1	9	0.1
Sikh	5	0.0	1	0.0	6	0.2	3	0.1	11	0.1	4	0.0
Hindu	4	0.0	1	0.0	1	0.0	1	0.0	5	0.0	2	0.0
Greek Orthodox	1	0.0	0	0.0	1	0.0	0	0.0	2	0.0	1	0.0
Quaker	1	0.0	0	0.0	0	0.0	0	0.0	1	0.0	0	0.0
Seventh Day Adventist	1	0.0	0	0.0	0	0.0	0	0.0	1	0.0	0	0.0
United Reformed Church	1	0.0	0	0.0	0	0.0	0	0.0	1	0.0	0	0.0
Faith schools (all)	6,176	36.8	1,266	29.0	637	18.8	579	18.9	6,813	33.8	1,845	24.7
Total	16,786	100.0	4,373	100.0	3,380	100.0	3,061	100.0	20,165	100.0	7,464	100.0

Note: Primary and secondary totals include middle schools. Secondary includes all-through schools.

Source: Long and Bolton (2017: 18).

Table 4.7: Primary, secondary, and all-age pupil numbers: schools in England, 2006–16

	State-funded primary schools	State-funded secondary schools	All school types (inc. independent schools)
2006	4,150,595	3,347,500	8,231,055
2007	4,110,750	3,325,625	8,167,715
2008	4,090,400	3,294,575	8,121,955
2009	4,077,350	3,278,130	8,092,280
2010	4,096,580	3,278,485	8,098,360
2011	4,137,755	3,262,635	8,123,865
2012	4,217,000	3,234,875	8,178,200
2013	4,309,580	3,210,120	8,249,810
2014	4,416,710	3,181,360	8,331,385
2015	4,510,310	3,184,730	8,438,145
2016	4,615,170	3,193,420	8,559,540

Source: DfE, 2016c: Main text, 3.

Table 4.8: Pupil numbers in state-funded schools in England, 2016

Type	Total
State-funded primary schools: full-time boys	2,214,581
State-funded primary schools: full-time girls	2,128,892
State-funded primary schools: part-time boys	137,517
State-funded primary schools: part-time girls	134,182
Total	*4,615,172*
State-funded secondary schools: full-time boys	1,603,077
State-funded secondary schools: full-time girls	1,587,068
State-funded secondary schools: part-time boys	1,674
State-funded secondary schools: part-time girls	1,599
Total	*3,193,418*
State-funded special schools: full-time boys	74,362
State-funded special schools: full-time girls	29,470
State-funded special schools: part-time boys	995
State-funded special schools: part-time girls	536
Total	*105,363*

Type	Total
Non-maintained special schools: full-time boys	2,746
Non-maintained special schools: full-time girls	1,031
Non-maintained special schools: part-time boys	27
Non-maintained special schools: full-time girls	10
Total	*3,814*
Overall total	*7,917,767*

Source: DfE, 2016c: National Tables, SFR20/2016, table 1a.

Table 4.9: School and pupil numbers by academy type, England, 2016

	Number of schools	Number of male pupils	Number of female pupils	Total
Primary converter academy	1,963	308,022	297,238	605,260
Primary sponsored academy	928	142,685	136,493	279,178
Primary free school	117	8,824	8,254	17,078
Secondary converter academy	1,408	758,043	769,404	1,527,447
Secondary sponsored academy	586	265,092	247,907	512,999
Secondary free school	135	22,560	19,411	41,971
University technical college	39	6,969	2,234	9,203
Studio school	37	2,690	2,017	4,707
Special converter academy	137	13,045	5,376	18,421
Special sponsored academy	28	1,575	496	2,071
Special free school	19	586	128	714
Alternative provision converter academy	32	1,270	525	1,795
Alternative provision sponsored academy	13	555	237	792
Alternative provision free school	32	712	329	1,041
Total	5,474	1,532,628	1,490,049	3,022,677

Source: DfE, 2016c: National Tables, SFR20/2016, table 2b.

There now exists a wide variety of schools in England (see Tables 4.7, 4.8, and 4.9). There are different types of academies, even if they all have the same legal status, as 'academies'. Academies are publicly funded independent schools, held accountable through legally binding agreements with the Department for Education. They have some freedoms from national curricula, school hours and term dates, and staff pay and conditions. Free schools, academy converters, and traditional academies have the same status, though there are a number of differences between them. Free schools are new state schools and include independent schools which have become financially unviable and are becoming state schools for the first time. They are set up by teachers, parents, educational charities, universities, and community groups, and conform in their governance structures to the Department for Education's model memorandum and articles of association. They are free from LEA control. Traditional academies typically have been underperforming existing schools, which are then allocated an academy sponsor. Academy sponsors come from the university, further education, charity, and business sectors. They are independent of the LEA. There is also a category of academy converters: these are typically high-performing schools according to some measure of achievement adopted by the Department for Education, who opt out of local authority control in order to gain greater independence and autonomy. University technical colleges and studio schools are academies for 14- to 19-year-olds. They are supported by employers to help them craft their curricula to prepare them for work.

At present, and even as the number of academies in England is increasing, the majority of state schools are maintained. This means that they are overseen by LEAs, or local authorities (LAs) as they have now become known. They are legally obligated to follow the national curriculum and abide by national teacher pay and conditions. There are four types of maintained schools: community, foundation and trust, voluntary aided, and voluntary controlled schools. Community schools are controlled and run by the local authority. The local authority employs the staff, owns the land and buildings, and determines the admissions arrangements. Foundation and trust schools are run by governing bodies. The land and buildings are usually owned by the governing body or, in the case of a trust school, a charity. The majority of voluntary aided schools are faith schools. A foundation or trust (sometimes but not always a religious organization) provides a small amount of capital costs and is given a majority of places on the school's governing body. The governing body employs the staff and decides on admissions criteria. The land and buildings are usually owned by the foundation or trust. Voluntary controlled schools are set up and run by LAs. However, a foundation or trust owns the land and buildings and appoints a quarter of the governing body.

Academies and maintained schools form the largest types of school in England. There are, however, two other types of schools: private or independent schools (see Chapter 2) and grammar schools (see earlier in this chapter). Grammar schools remain state funded and have a selective intake. Independent schools charge fees and are allowed by statutory law to make a profit. They are lightly regulated by government and inspected by a range of bodies that they have set up themselves. They are funded by fees, gifts, and endowments and are governed by an independently elected board of governors.

Both Conservative and Labour governments over the last forty years have campaigned and legislated for choice mechanisms. This necessarily entails establishing and maintaining a variety of schools, and this has been the rationale for the heterogeneity of the school sector. Discourses frame political agendas. Norman Fairclough (2000), for example, suggests that the UK Labour government between 1997 and 2010 developed an educational agenda that was underpinned by a combination of a social integrationist discourse, with the focus on shifting people from welfare to work, and a moral underclass discourse. He argues that there are three possible ways of framing notions of equality as a political discourse. The first of these is a redistributionist discourse, which focuses on reducing poverty by redistributing wealth. A second discourse is socially integrationist in form, and here exclusion is primarily caused by unemployment and other social problems, with the solution being to reduce high levels of unemployment and get people into work. The third discourse, a moral underclass discourse, is perhaps more foundational, in so far as deficiencies are identified as existing in the culture and experiences of those who are excluded, with the solution to this being cultural change and the imposition of education programmes to facilitate inclusion. This last is therefore very much a deficit model, which focuses on the right ways of behaving in society, rather than on specific outcomes from particular socio-economic arrangements. The New Labour governments of the late twentieth and early twenty-first centuries were also attracted by communitarian thinking, which attempted to link three themes: economic efficiency, social cohesion, and morality. It is important to highlight, especially in relation to political discourses, the ephemeral and non-binding nature of discursive constructions.

UK Conservative government policy after 2010 was more concerned with issues surrounding the erosion of responsibility in society, caused, as their political representatives repeatedly stressed, by an overwhelming paternalistic state. The prime minister at this time, David Cameron, argued for a collective culture of responsibility and an ethos of self-betterment. The state in this vision has two principal roles: the efficient delivery of public services, and early life interventions, achieved through paternalistic nudges to the populace (described by others as 'guided choice' strategies). If this doesn't work then the state is forced to mobilize its repressive resources to ensure the good order of society, and these punitive measures can take the form either of the withdrawal of goods usually provided by the state or of restrictions on people's freedom.

These policies and practices have therefore contributed to greater levels of inequality in the system, though the education sector cannot be held responsible for all the types of inequality (of goods, of opportunities, and of life conditions) that exist in England at the present time. The next chapter focuses on the assessment and examination practices that have in a variety of ways created and recreated forms of inequality in a country such as England.

Chapter 5

Examination and testing

There have been four significant changes to pedagogic and professional practices in the English education system in the last thirty years. The first of these refers to the professional status of teachers, which has implications for the types of power flows that operate within the system. The teaching profession in the UK has since 1988, when the Education Reform Act was passed, experienced changing relations with the state, professional fragmentation, and a reconceptualization of its ideological ethos. Before 1988 the teaching profession had a degree of autonomy from the state, which meant that it was able to shape its direction to some degree. It was able to do this in relation to the particular ideal of service it subscribed to, the specific nature of the discourse community that was established, the distinctive epistemology of practice to which it worked, and the control it exercised over the development and maintenance of its specialized body of knowledge. If these four infrastructural elements change in response to the needs of the state and through the policy cycle in which the state takes a dominant role, then this constitutes a loss of control that the profession can exercise over its core business. Indeed, the decline of the professional authority of the teaching profession in England since 1988 has been extensively documented (e.g. Smyth, 2001). This would suggest that the teaching body in England should now be characterized as a state-regulated rather than a licensed occupation.

A second change to the teaching profession in England during this period has been the fragmentation of its professional remit. This is best exemplified by the way head teachers and teachers are increasingly being understood as different types of professionals, each of them having different sets of competences, different relations with the state and quasi-governmental bodies, and indeed different relations with each other. New head teachers in the maintained sector are now required to have a national qualification, delivered and accredited by the National College for Teaching and Leadership, before they can be appointed. The overall effect of these changes has been to managerialize the head teacher role. From a situation where the head teacher was understood as a leading teacher, the role has now changed to one of managing teacher performance. As a result different lists ...itudes have been developed for head teachers and teachers, and this has led to a fragmentation of the profession and a distancing in professional terms of teachers from managers. Further to this, schools are now seen as service cost centres in a quasi-market system, which compete for pupils with each other, and understand the direction of their accountability as being to governments, quasi-governmental bodies, and parents, rather than to the teaching profession as a whole.

A third change to the professional mandate of teachers in England concerns the way pre-service and in-service training is now regulated by governments and quasi-governmental bodies, with, as we saw in Chapter 3, some pre-service training programmes now being delivered at the school level. At the pre-service level, university providers are required to conform to a code as to what they can teach and how it can be taught, and this is formally inspected by the national inspection body, the Office for Standards in Education, Children's Services and Skills (Ofsted), which has the power to withdraw that licence from providers.

And the fourth of these changes has been a rescripting of the notions of quality and service, and consequently, new positions, roles, and sets of moral ordinances for the workforce. Ball (2008) suggests that in addition to the new forms of managerialism that were introduced into schools during this period, there has been a greater emphasis on performativity. This is 'a technology, a culture and a mode of regulation that employs judgments, comparisons and displays as a means of incentive, control, attrition and change' (ibid.: 216). Performativity requires measurements of staff productivity and employs rewards and sanctions to guide staff performance to meet organizational goals. While professionalism and performativity may share the same goals – for example improvements in performance – their cultures and discourses are fundamentally different.

The post-war consensus about the curriculum in maintained schools reflected a settlement between the various stakeholders as to its contents (and the relations between the different elements), its mode of accountability, and its delivery. Schools in both the primary and secondary sectors were not thought of as accountable to governments for the curriculum that they followed and what this meant was that they were not required to justify the curricular decisions they made to policy makers, where these referred to the contents of this curriculum or the consequences of following it. (In reality, different forms of control operated, but these were between different people and allocated different amounts of power to the different partners.) For a long period of time after the Second World War, schools were relatively independent of government and parental pressures with regard to these matters. Control structures were of a professional kind, with schools organizing their activities on the basis of their own presumed expertise in curriculum and pedagogy. (This still operates in the private sector, though market forces are holding these schools to account through a results-based mechanism, however unreliable this might be.) After this post-war consensus broke down, a national curriculum was introduced (which over time has been extensively revised, with more and more exemptions to it allowed), accountability relations between the different parts of the system were changed, and a different type of account was now required.

Four mechanisms of accountability can be identified: a central control model (including an evaluative state model), a quasi-market model, a professional expert model, and a partnership model. Professional development and partnership models have gradually been eroded within the English education system and been replaced by statist, evaluative-statist, and quasi-market models of accountability. And this has had profound effects on the discursive spaces that teachers now inhabit. These mechanisms have different characteristics and dimensions, and they can be understood as positions on a number of scales: the degree to which they engender a low or high level of trust within the system; the degree of punitive strength they can muster; their capacity to influence the activities under scrutiny, for example whether they can or cannot initiate washback effects; their capacity to influence the epistemological character of the setting; the degree of affordance they give to participants in the setting; and their underpinning ideological framework regarding human nature and possible forms of human interaction.

Assessment

Perhaps the most significant change to the English education system over the last thirty years occurred through devaluations and revaluations of the currency of education for schools, teachers, and students. This happened because successive governments, both Labour and Conservative, drove through assessment-led reforms, with subsequent effects on curriculum, governance, quality assurance, learning, and accountability. In the context of the introduction of the national curriculum in England, it is possible to identify a number of seminal phases or interventions by governments or government bodies with regard to assessment and evaluation. These refer to the means by which teachers, schools, and students are judged.

The first of these found its most direct expression in the Task Group on Assessment and Testing (TGAT) Report commissioned by the government in 1988 (DES, 1988a), which argued that the fundamental building blocks of any national assessment system should be regular cycles of teacher assessments and that these should be fully integrated with teaching and learning programmes. The report proposed a ten-level system to encourage progression, with the average pupil expected to change levels every two years. In addition, it recommended the adoption of a criterion-referenced framework so that children's achievements could be assessed against inscribed levels of criteria. The authors of the report signalled their opposition to assessments that were separate from and not connected to curricula, and yet, at the same time, argued that results should be published at the end of each key stage without being adjusted for the socio-economic background of individuals and schools.

At the second phase a number of significant changes to these original recommendations were made. These downgraded the importance of teacher assessments, with the reasoning being that teachers could not be trusted to mark their students fairly because they had a vested interest in the results. This low trust approach was to become a defining characteristic of the reforms and system interventions. What this meant was that the connection between these forms of assessment conducted at the end of the four key stages and the teaching and learning programmes associated with them was weakened. Formal assessments conducted at the end of each key stage became the norm. The report also recommended that teacher assessments should cover those attainment targets that could not be covered by Standard Assessment Tasks (SATs), with these being designated as mechanisms for deciding at which level pupils would be entered.

The third phase, which coincided with the appointment of a new secretary of state, was a continuation of the direction established in phase two. Instead of Standard Assessment Tasks, which were long, interactive, curriculum-focused, and had formative potential, the development agencies were instructed to deliver 'paper and pencil', summative, easily managed, and simpler to process end-of-key-stage tests. At the same time, coursework components in the national system of examination at the age of 16, known as the General Certificate of Secondary Education (at key stage 4), were to be statutorily reduced, and publication of test scores, which were not modified by value-added processes, received legislative endorsement in the 1994 Education Act.

The fourth phase culminated in the Dearing Review (DES, 1993, 1994), which recommended separating out formative and summative forms of assessment, repositioning on an equal basis teacher assessments and Standard Assessment Tasks, replacing the ten-level system with four separate reporting stages, and slimming down the curriculum as well as these assessment arrangements.

The fifth phase was a period of consolidation and refinement, though much of the work done by governments during this period entailed trimming, adapting, and compromising at the level of detail. The building blocks of the assessment-driven reform processes were already in place and were not significantly amended after this. However, productive forms of pedagogy need assessment to be congruent with learning. The problem then is that the same assessment is not able to both contribute to the development of learning and in addition determine whether learning has actually taken place. Different assessment processes are required to perform these two functions. This has been the key misconstrual in UK policy and practice over the last thirty years.

The first phase, then, focused on the publication of the TGAT Report in 1988 (DES, 1988a), followed by three supplements (DES, 1988b) a few months later. TGAT argued that a fully integrated system of assessment can and should be both formative and summative:

> Promoting children's learning is the principal aim of school. Assessment lies at the heart of this process. It can provide a framework in which educational objectives may be set and pupils' progress charted and expressed. It can yield a basis for planning the next educational steps in response to children's needs. By facilitating dialogue between teachers, it can enhance professional skills and help the school as a whole to strengthen learning across the curriculum and throughout its age range.
>
> (DES, 1988a: 23)

Later changes to the assessment arrangements have focused on unpicking this apparent conflation within the same system of these two purposes (either by downgrading the one at the expense of the other, such as in phase three, or clearly separating the different purposes, as Dearing (1993) suggested, in phase four).

Formative modes of assessment are most closely associated with the process of teaching itself, but it is the results of summative tests that are most visible and public. Formative dimensions of assessment focus on providing information for the teacher about the way learners complete particular tasks. The information provided is intended to feed directly into the teaching process, so the focus is on how students tackle these tasks and how they go about solving problems that they are given. The assessment environment does not need to be standardized during formative processes of assessment.

Summative assessment is concerned with determining whether students have mastered particular elements of the curriculum. Summative assessments aim to be reliable and valid; homogeneity of context is considered to be important so that comparison becomes possible. A summative assessment marks some point in the otherwise potentially organic teaching and learning process at which it is decided to stop teaching and give one's full attention to assessment. The stage at which it is most important to carry out this kind of assessment is often determined by factors other than those arising from learning goals, such as predetermined times in the school year, or a requirement to report to other interested parties.

TGAT further argued that assessments should be connected with and not separated from curricula:

> The assessment system being proposed differs from most of the standardized testing that is now used in many primary schools and some secondary schools. Those tests are not related closely to what children are being taught, and when they identify children likely to have difficulties they give little indication of the nature of problems. Their purpose is to compare children with each other and with samples of children with whom the tests were originally developed, often many years ago.
>
> (DES, 1988a: 97)

Assessments may be more or less integrated with the teaching programmes that pupils follow. Some kinds of assessment (e.g. IQ tests) are not designed to measure pupils' learning (or the results of a teaching programme), in which case they are often associated with measures of qualities supposedly inherent in the student, such as intelligence. Assessment which is placed at the integrated end of the continuum is likely to be more informal than formal, more formative than summative, process-oriented rather than product-oriented, and to be frequent or continuous rather than taking place at one time point, usually at the end of the programme of study.

TGAT (ibid.) advocated a criterion-referenced system of assessment:

> In which an award or grade is made on the basis of the quality of the performance of the pupil, irrespective of the performance of other pupils . . . [so] that teachers and pupils [can] be given clear descriptions of the performances being sought.
>
> (DES, 1988a: 97)

Though norm-referenced systems of assessment have become less popular, criterion-referenced systems are not without their problems. Systems with a simple pass/fail result, such as a driving test, are much easier to operate than complex multi-level systems such as a national curriculum. Criteria are relatively easy to identify for use in testing a performance like driving proficiency, but harder to associate precisely with a range of levels of learning as in a national curriculum. In addition, criterion-referenced systems conflate logical hierarchies of skill and content with developmental approaches to the teaching of students. Finally, establishing criteria appropriate to the various levels involves some notion of an average student, which is always difficult to determine.

Another element of the assessment scheme proposed by TGAT concerned arrangements for reporting. The task force recommended that there should be no obligation on a school or a local education authority to publish information about the results of the assessments made at key stage 1. At the other key stages (2, 3, and 4), TGAT suggested that unmodified data should be published, albeit '[o]nly if this is done in the context of reports about that school as a whole, so that it can be fair to that school's work and take account so far as possible of socio-economic and other influences' (DES, 1988a: 99).

The arguments against this approach and in favour of a value-added approach have been well-rehearsed, both with regard to theoretical issues and practice. (The latest manifestation of the attempt to assess value added is Progress 8, which is likely to be replaced sooner or later by another attempt to reconcile the irreconcilable, the learning and accountability functions of an educational mechanism.) However, at the time of the TGAT Report's publication it quickly became official policy to publish raw examination performance data in league (or alphabetically arranged) tables, without reference to the school's socio-economic profile in the form of any general statement. TGAT thus attempted to combine different functions of assessment, incorporated different models of school improvement, and supported conflicting notions of accountability.

Two models of assessment can be identified and, as we have seen, both were present to some extent in the TGAT Report, though they are contradictory. The first of these models suggests that ideas and information gathered during an assessment process can be used by teachers and students to plan future learning experiences. Assessment as part of a school improvement process is perceived as *contextualized* (the timing of the assessments, their relationships to the specifics of the course, and the conditions under which they are undertaken are all taken into consideration as teachers, parents, and children interpret the results); as *ipsative* (where the assessments refer only to the teaching and learning profiles of those students and their past achievements, with comparisons with other students and schools not being drawn from them); and as *non-competitive* (where this emphasizes a professional commitment to high standards of teaching rather than a competitive incentive to outperform other students, teachers, or schools). More importantly, this model places a low emphasis on external accountability, whether in the context of free-market consumerism or state control systems of accountability. Accountability may be directly to the students, but as a mode of professionalism rather than a response to external pressures. The alternative model characterizes assessment as *decontextualized*. Here, a high emphasis is placed on comparability, so that variables particular to specific students, teaching situations, or schools are not given the same priority as they are in the first model. Assessment is also perceived as *competitive*: a teacher's work is judged in relation to the achievements of his or her peers. Lastly, this model strongly emphasizes *external accountability*. Indeed, in line with a free-market consumerist model of accountability, failure in the context of the public marketplace leads to a loss of income for the school and of employment for teachers. Aspects of both models featured in the initial TGAT Report, though subsequent arrangements made for assessment are more in line with the second model. It was thus hardly surprising that the contents of the TGAT Report were interpreted in different ways by different people. Some pointed to its progressive features, others identified those of a more regressive nature.

TGAT made a number of recommendations about the role and importance of teacher assessments. The chief purpose of the SATs was to ensure reliability and comparability, and furthermore it was suggested that these should work at the class and not the individual level. If they diverged, the teacher assessment was adjusted. In phase two the School Examinations and Assessment Council (SEAC) proposed in response to the TGAT Report that:

> First, teachers would assess pupils on every attainment target... Subject scores would be aggregated and passed onto local moderators in the spring. Second, teachers would administer SATs in the summer to all pupils 'but possibly only for some attainment targets'. Where available, the SAT result would displace the teacher assessment.
>
> (SEAC, 1989a: 68)

SEAC went further at the end of the year in making the following recommendations to the secretary of state:

1. By the end of the spring term preceding the end of the key stage there should be a recorded teacher assessment giving the level each pupil had reached in each attainment target.
2. When the SATs have been used in the summer term there will also be a recorded SAT outcome for some attainment targets – probably not all.
3. Where (1) and (2) yield the same outcome for each profile component, that is the end of the matter. The SAT outcome for the attainment, where there is one, should stand.
4. Where (1) and (2) yield a different outcome for any profile component, the SAT outcome may be used for the pupil record if the teacher is content. If the teacher believes (1) should be used, the teacher will be required to make a case for this choice through local moderating arrangements, details of which still await clarification.

(SEAC, 1989a: 68–9)

These proposals formed part of the final standing orders published in July 1990. They also included complicated rules for aggregating attainment target achievements, and aggregating profile achievements into subject achievements.

The new orders signalled a radical change of direction. Henceforth, assessment, moderation, and reporting would operate at the level of individual attainment targets. More importantly, Standard Assessment Tasks were to be the principal method of assessment, with teacher assessments being marginalized. Assessment arrangements in this phase were in a state of transition, with no clear ideological line as yet forthcoming. What was also beginning to emerge was a desire by the central authority to reinforce and augment government control modes of accountability. In phase three the trend became clearer.

In 1990 a new secretary of state, Kenneth Clarke, took over. He was determined to reassert the power of the central authority over its constituent bodies. He wanted to limit and circumscribe the power of the individual teacher, 'the professional expert', by reordering relations between the different parts of the system. He inherited a number of problems: for example, the first Standard Assessment Tasks appeared to be too long, too detailed, and difficult to manage. They also required considerable input by teachers, with the result that doubts began to be expressed about their reliability and comparability. It was also suggested at this time that standards were being eroded in the GCSE exams taken by pupils at the end of key stage 4, as the number of candidates obtaining high grades increased each year. The secretary of state reacted in two ways. First, a number of development contracts for key stage 3 Standard Assessment Tasks were terminated, and new specifications were set in place. These required the Mathematics Development Agency, for example, to produce at key stage 3 a set of three one-hour tests covering all the content attainment targets. Process attainment tasks were to be assessed by non-statutory Standard Assessment Tasks, and there was a general revision and culling of attainment targets. The effect of this type of testing was problematic: it limited the capacity of the assessments to allow formative and diagnostic judgements to be made; it further separated assessment processes from applications of curricula by restricting and standardizing the way these assessments were made; and it downgraded the importance of teacher assessments.

A similar move occurred with coursework arrangements in the GCSE. Political rhetoric here emphasized reliability, comparability, and the maintenance of standards. The secretary of state argued that:

> Coursework should play an important part in its curriculum, but not all of it is good. SEAC and HMI have constantly identified cases in which there is too much variation in the tasks set, too much diversity in marking and moderation, and too much opportunity for cheating. It may not give a true and honest indication of a pupil's ability.
>
> (Clarke, 1991: 2)

From 1994, the maximum amount of coursework allowed was: English 40 per cent, mathematics 20 per cent, science 30 per cent, technology 60 per cent, history 25 per cent, geography 25 per cent, social science 20 per cent, business studies 25 per cent, and economics 20 per cent. Twenty years later, coursework is now even more restricted in most subjects, including those that have practical elements.

Phase three, then, represents the clearest expression of what has been called a 'standards and accountability' model. In particular this phase saw a considerable emphasis being placed on the publishing of league and alphabetically arranged tables of performance, with the unit of currency unadjusted. This and other aspects of the testing arrangements would lead to a boycott by the teacher unions, with few schools completing the key stage 3 statutory tests in the summer of 1993 and a significant number of primary and infant schools abandoning key stage 1 assessments halfway through their administration. The ability of the central authority to impose its agenda on schools was being challenged. The response by government was to commission the Dearing Review (1993), culminating in the Dearing Report (1994), and this constituted phase four.

The Dearing Report (1994) sought to bridge the divide between the competing parties. Dearing then proposed a number of significant amendments (TGAT, 1998b). Although he accepted the need to separate teacher assessments from national test results by recommending that they 'should be shown separately in all forms of reporting and in school prospectuses' (1994: 52), he also argued for those teacher assessments to be moderated in terms of statutory end-of-key-stage tests. Depending on the means used, this could have resulted in two sets of results being reported side-by-side, with similarities and differences between them being open for discussion. What Dearing was trying to do here was separate out formative and diagnostic purposes of assessment from summative and evaluative ones. However, this had the effect of reasserting the importance of teacher assessments, although his recommendation was that they should be moderated externally by Standard Assessment Tasks (SATs).

Dearing further proposed that the prescribed curricular arrangements as they had been expressed in the published orders should be cut back. The time released would allow the teaching of non-statutory material, the teaching of programmes of study which would go beyond those laid down in the new orders, the teaching of subjects not included in the national curriculum, and the reinforcing of basic skills. Though the time left would still be small in relation to the time spent on the prescribed curriculum, this would significantly affect the ability of teachers to contribute to curriculum-making and thus allow them to be responsive to the needs of their pupils.

Another suggestion that Dearing made was that the ten-level system should be replaced by four separate age-related systems. The intention was clear: to simplify and clarify, and thus to make workable, these assessment arrangements. He argued that the ten-level system had three problematic aspects: subject knowledge and skills are not necessarily best expressed in a linear form; pupils do not necessarily learn best in simple, orderly, and linear ways; and 'it is difficult to devise clear, unambiguous, hierarchical criteria except for simple or clearly defined tasks' (Dearing, 1994: 40).

Finally he argued for a need to collect and publish summative data about pupils and schools. He was sympathetic about the need to rework the unmodified data to allow for socio-economic factors to be taken into account, and he rejected the arguments for carefully devised light sampling to allow judgements to be made about the system year by year. So, while separating out formative and summative forms of assessment, he in fact aligned closely together these functions and thus placed this alignment within a standards and accountability model. This is further evidence of the tensions between two conflicting models of accountability. The first of these emphasizes professional control over curricula, though teachers would be expected to respond to the demands of external review. The second is a variant on the consumerist model, in which market mechanisms predominate and data are gathered to compare schools with each other. If those data reflect badly on particular schools, then the market exacts a penalty; the school loses pupils and teachers and may even have to close down.

The Dearing reforms effectively set in place the form that national curriculum assessments would take for the next 20 years (phase five). The early part of the New Labour government's twelve-year period in office saw the development of national literacy and numeracy strategies at the primary school level. These were perceived to be successful, though later analyses suggested that exaggerated claims had been made about them, especially at key stage 3 (Coe and Tymms, 2008). However, it was becoming increasingly apparent that the publication mechanism was becoming of greater significance, as ministers embraced the target culture and as the Ofsted inspection process began to use such data to make judgements about schools, which had real effects on the survival of those schools. These judgements were comparative in two senses: against a benchmark, so that expected proportions of children achieving a certain level became established within the system; and the translation of these (with other observational data collected) to categorize schools into successful or failing ones, with severe consequences for those schools which didn't reach acceptable standards.

This change of tactics took a further sudden step in October 2008, when the secretary of state for education, Ed Balls, unexpectedly announced the cessation of national curriculum testing at key stage 3, with immediate effect. This included scrapping both the existing key stage tests and the single-level tests, which would continue to be piloted for key stage 2 only. In making this announcement, the secretary of state set out the government's view of three key principles for the continuation of the assessment system. He said that it should, first, give parents the information they would need to compare different schools, choose the right school for their child, and then track their child's progress; second, enable head teachers and teachers to secure the progress of every child and their school as a whole, without unnecessary burdens or bureaucracy; and third, allow the public to hold national and local government and governing bodies to account for the performance of schools. The tensions and contradictions within this assessment model are glaringly obvious. In light of these principles, the secretary of state said that key stage 3 testing was not justified. Parents could obtain information from GCSE results, and a new system of 'real-time reporting of progress' would be developed for tracking individual pupils. It amounted to very little and was repeatedly replaced over the next few years by new and different types of value-added arrangements, none of which was more successful than those they replaced. In addition, there would also be an externally marked test with a sample of pupils to measure national performance, holding the government to account. Adjustments were made to this testing and accountability regime in the years that followed and up to the present; however, the principle of testing remained intact. The most significant of all the changes initiated by successive governments in England over the last thirty years has been these assessment reforms: their power is such that the various systems of curriculum, pedagogy, learning, teaching, and school governance have all been influenced by them.

Education in England has gone through many changes in the last three decades, among them an increase in standardization, regulation, and auditing of the education system. While the social status of teachers had declined, there is an increasing awareness that teachers are the essential factor for educational quality. As a result an increased emphasis is put on initial qualifications and continuous professional development of teachers and principals, as indicated by the development of qualified teacher status (QTS) and the National Professional Qualification for Headship (NPQH). However, the focus on accountability and evaluation of performance has generally led to a marginalization of areas that are not and cannot be assessed. Social class remains the key variable associated with educational participation and opportunity in the UK. There is a significant reproduction of status and education within families across generations.

Successive governments have driven through assessment-led reforms, with consequences for curriculum, governance, notions of quality, learning, and accountability. The main features of these reforms have been to introduce high-stakes testing and external forms of control. Education professionals at all levels are required to provide numerical evidence to show how they perform, and this is expressed as indicators of effectiveness. Rewards and sanctions based on these numerical indicators are designed to put pressure on school managers and teachers. The expectations and roles of school principals and teachers are reduced to targets and numbers, instead of the quality of teaching and the quality of the learning experience. School principals increasingly see themselves as managers who interpret and manipulate these numbers. Teachers teach curriculum content that is relevant to standardized testing, focusing on improving test results. The curriculum is narrowed while students are drilled to master tests. This technocratic school culture disengages teachers from high-quality teaching and a commitment to shared practice. The curriculum model that emerged from these reforms was generally subject-orientated, fragmented, and linear, and prioritized summative assessment processes. These reforms also contributed to various forms of inequality, in relation to our three types: inequality of goods, inequality of opportunities to obtain these goods, and inequality of life conditions.

Comparisons with other countries

What was also significant about this time-period in the development and evolution of the English education system was the formation of cross-national systems of testing and assessment, with consequent implications for knowledge development within the system and about it. Andreas Schleicher (2015), from the Organisation for Economic Co-operation and Development (OECD) and with regard to the Programme for International Student Assessment (PISA), uses a methodology that involves the ranking of a number of countries in relation to their performance on a series of tests, and then the identification of those systemic elements that are present in high-performing countries and not present in low-performing countries. From this he concludes that it is possible to identify the optimum conditions for a system's effectiveness. He is therefore able to suggest that: children from similar social backgrounds can show very different performance levels, depending on the school they go to or the country they live in; there is no relationship between the share of students with an immigrant background in a country and the overall performance of students in that country; there is no relation between class size and learning outcomes within or across countries (the conceptual framework he applies here makes the unjustified assumption that all the different types of learning activities are optimally performed with the same class size); there is no incompatibility between the quality of learning and equity, since the highest-performing education systems combine both; all students are capable of achieving high standards; and, more generally, top-performing education systems tend to be more rigorous, with fewer curriculum items and with those that are included being taught in greater depth.

The approach has a number of flaws in its conceptualization and application. The first of these is that an assumption is made that a person has a knowledge, skill, or dispositional set, which is configured in a particular way (i.e. it has a grammar), and it is this knowledge, skill, or dispositional set, or at least one or more elements of it, which is directly assessed when that person is tested. In contrast, any testing that is carried out with the purpose of determining whether these attributes are held, not held, or even partially held by an individual always involves an indirect process of examination, where the additional element is a conjecture, retroduction, inference, or best guess.

A second false belief is that this grammar is organized into elements, that there are relations between those elements, and each element can be scaled, which can then be directly investigated. This can be contrasted with a position which suggests that, in the application of the knowledge, skill, or dispositional set, whether for the purposes of testing or for use in everyday life, a range of other knowledge elements, skills, and dispositions are referred to. There is, therefore, a set of factors that in combination may result in construct-irrelevance variance (Messick, 1989) – that is, variance amongst a population of testees as a result of factors that do not have anything to do with the construct being tested. Even if knowledge of or competence in the construct is equally distributed in this population, some testees will do better than others (i.e. on their actual scores) for reasons other than because they have greater knowledge of or are more competent in the construct being tested. This might involve either construct-underrepresentation or construct-overrepresentation (Wiliam, 2011), and within the confines of the test itself it is impossible to determine which of these has occurred.

A third false belief is that in the use of a knowledge set, or in the performance of a skill, or in the application of a disposition, no internal transformation takes place. In fact there is also an external transformative process at work, and thus a fourth false belief is that testing a person's knowledge, skills, and aptitudes has no washback effects on either the original knowledge construct, or the internally transformed knowledge set ready for testing. In contrast, the well-documented process of washback works in just this way (Stobart, 2008), so that instead of the assessment acting merely as a descriptive device, it also acts in a variety of ways to transform the construct it is seeking to measure.

A fifth false belief is that the process of testing works in a unidirectional linear fashion. For example, a person knows something, that person is subjected to a test which is designed to test for traces of that learning in a population of knowers with similar characteristics, and a score in relation to that construct is recorded indicating that the person either knows it, doesn't know it, or knows it to some extent. No consideration is given to bidirectionality, incorporating forward and backward flows, so that the taking of the test and the recording of the mark impact on and influence the original knowledge construct. This changes the structure (both quantitatively and qualitatively) of the construct, and its affordances, making the original determination of it and them unreliable.

A sixth false belief is that different types of knowledge, including those at different levels of abstraction, can be tested using the same algorithmic process; and a seventh false belief is that the performance on the test represents to a greater or lesser extent (given that the person may have been distracted or constrained in some way or another) what the testee can do or show, rather than there being a qualitative difference between the performance on the test and the construct, skill, or disposition of the testee. An individual may have to reframe his or her knowledge set to fit the test, and therefore the assessment of their mastery of the construct is not a determination of their capacity in relation to the original construct, but a determination of whether they have successfully understood how to rework their capacity to fit the demands of the testing technology.

An eighth false belief is that a test can be constructed which is culture-free or free of those issues that disadvantage some types of learners at the expense of others. The extent of cultural bias in the PISA tests is unrealized and certainly underreported. In addition, a particular technical problem with PISA relates to its sampling procedures. If different types of sampling are used across the different countries, then some of these countries will be disadvantaged compared with others. Sampling issues are present in any test, whether they involve the selection of children from a number of grade levels without specifying proportions from each grade, selecting only a certain part of a country for reporting purposes and ignoring the rest (as in the latest PISA tests (OECD, 2015), where only the richest and better educated cohort of learners (from Shanghai) was entered, and these were allowed to represent China as a whole), or the selective non-participation of some types of schools in some countries and not others. Cultural differences take a number of different forms, such as ascribing different values (and different strengths of values) to cultural items, or determining the nature, quality, probative force, relevance-value, and extent of evidence, or focusing on practices which may be more familiar to people in some countries and less so in others. However, more importantly, cultural difference with regard to the selection of test items refers to the expression of the problem to be solved. If, for example, different national idioms, different national ways of thinking embedded in language forms, and different normic values woven into the fabric of national discourses are ignored, then the presentation of the actual test items as well as the range of possible answers that can be given may favour students from one nation at the expense of students from another.

There are a number of ways of identifying good practice within a system of education. The first is identifying outputs from the system (these can be test scores, dispositional elements, acquired skills, ethical and moral qualities); that is, outputs that have resulted from the individual's participation in the system itself. The argument is then made that one system is better than another, because it has better outputs, and further to this that the characteristics of these national systems should be bottled up and transferred wholesale to those countries or jurisdictions which are considered not to be as successful or effective in these terms.

If the information collected about individuals in a system of education at the end of their time spent in the system is used to make judgements about the quality of provision within that system, then there are two possibilities for the type of information to be collected. The first is raw scores; in such an approach student scores are aggregated to allow comparative judgements to be made about these schools, districts, states, or nation states. The second is value-added scores; here, value-added data analysis models the input of particular institutions or systems, such as schools, in relation to the development of individuals that belong to those institutions or systems. As a result of these processes, a value can be attached to the input of the educational institution or nation as it has impacted upon the progress of the individual(s) who attended it, or have been part of it. The accuracy of such modelling depends on the belief that the educational researcher has in the reliability and validity of the data used, in the decisions they make about which variables to use in the modelling process, and also in the ability of the researcher to develop appropriate indicators or quasi-properties to reflect the actual properties of individuals, educational institutions, and nations, and their covariance in real-life settings. This in theory allows one to make comparative judgements between students, schools, districts, states, or nation states, though all the systems that have been devised and used have in one way or another proved to be unsatisfactory, and this includes the latest version, Progress 8.

A further way of determining quality in a system is by identifying a norm so as to allow a comparison to be made. For example, a system of education, whether international, national, or local, can be compared with, and marked against, a model of best practice, where this model is constructed in terms of the inclusion of all the possible elements that could and should form an education system (i.e. structures, institutions, curricula, pedagogic arrangements, and evaluative procedures), their arrangement in the most logical way (e.g. that curricular intentions should precede pedagogical approaches, which should, indeed, derive their credibility from these curricular intentions), and the identification and enactment of logically formed relational arrangements between these elements (i.e. that evaluative washback mechanisms should not be allowed to distort the curriculum as it was originally conceived). The norm that is used comparatively is constructed on sound logical and philosophical foundational principles. And in addition the meaning of concepts is treated as an empirical matter, as to how they are used in communities. A reliance on outputs in the comparative process is unsafe and, more importantly, likely to be invalid. The preferred methodological approach then becomes a searching for mechanisms, relations, and structures that are potentially causally efficacious, can be contextualized (historically, culturally, and socio-economically), and can also contribute to human wellbeing. And in turn this would involve the avoidance of reductionist and decontextualized accounts (such as in Barber *et al.*, 2007) of how education systems round the world operate.

The UK's performance in these PISA rankings has throughout the various iterations of the process remained relatively stable. The UK is consistently outranked by a number of other countries such as South Korea, Singapore, parts of China, and Finland (see Table 5.1).

Table 5.1: UK placement in PISA league tables, 2015

	Science	Reading	Mathematics
Mean score	509	498	492
League table ranking	15	22=	25=

Source: OECD, 2015.

Various governments have claimed that standards have improved in English schools as a result of policies they have developed and implemented, though in general they show high levels of grade inflation. In the next chapter we examine the issue of dis-ability.

ᴐns and demarcations:
ility and sexuality

The term *specific learning difficulties* refers to a range of learning difficulties experienced by children in English schools and tends to be used as a portmanteau word to include dyslexia, dyspraxia, dyscalculia, and the like. In the past these pupils were referred to as educationally subnormal or mentally handicapped, with these terms pointing to cognitive impairments as their source. The boundaries between those who were cognitively impaired and those who were not were strongly maintained, and this resulted in these children suffering forms of stigmatization and ridicule, which extended as well to those with physical dis-abilities. Donald Trump, the President of the United States, during the recent presidential election campaign, mocked a reporter with arthrogryposis, a congenital condition affecting his joints. The then Republican candidate gave an impression of the reporter, by waving his arms about in an exaggerated way, mocking and reviling him because he asked a difficult question. When confronted with this behaviour, Trump is reported to have said: '(h)e should stop using his disability to grandstand and get back to reporting for a paper that is rapidly going down the tubes'. The Warnock Report of 1978, conscious of the power of words and gestures in shaping the discursive landscape, sought to replace these terms with a general notion of learning difficulties. This acted against claims that abnormal cognitive functioning was the principal cause of difficulties in learning and allowed other explanations to be put forward. The 1981 Education Act mandated that a pupil was designated with special educational needs when they experienced significant difficulties in learning in comparison with their peers and when they had a dis-ability which limited access to educational environments.

In 1994, the Department for Education produced a code of practice, which offered guidance on the notion of specific learning difficulties:

> Some children may have significant difficulties in reading, writing, spelling or manipulating number, which are not typical of their general level of performance. They may gain some skills in some subjects quickly and demonstrate a high level of ability orally, yet may encounter sustained difficulty in gaining literacy and

numeracy skills. Such children can become severely frustrated and may also have emotional and/or behavioural difficulties.

(DfE, 1994: 67)

These definitions, however, tend to explain specific learning difficulties in deficit terms, and this has the potential to result in misleading understandings of learners' actual skills and abilities. The 2001 Code of Practice consolidated the concept into one overall definition, even though this then incorporated a large number of observed practices. In the Code the preferred term became 'special educational needs', with 'specific learning difficulties' being understood as a sub-category of this more general term (DfES, 2001). The Code suggested the following:

> Children have special educational needs if they have a learning difficulty, which calls for special educational provision to be made for them. Children have a learning difficulty if they: a) have a significantly greater difficulty in learning than the majority of children of the same age; or (b) have a disability which prevents or hinders them from making use of educational facilities of a kind generally provided for children of the same age in schools within the area of the local education authority; (c) are under compulsory school age and fall within the definition at (a) or (b) above or would so do if special educational provision was not made for them. Children must not be regarded as having a learning difficulty solely because the language or form of language of their home is different from the language in which they will be taught.
>
> (DfES, 2001: 6)

Although this definition referred to an extensive range of learning difficulties, what it didn't do was provide a precise definition of a learning difficulty. Despite this endorsement of pupils' sameness in learning, individual learning profiles were understood in terms of difference, and in particular, differences in the level and characteristics of specific learning difficulties, namely short-term working memory and organizational difficulties.

This meant that a number of terms were being used, which had different effects and consequences: special educational needs; pupils in need of special support; special needs; barriers to learning and participation, and so forth. It should also be noted that this naming approach may have had the effect of labelling and socially stigmatizing certain groups of children, though other practices, such as different table locations within the classroom and supportive mechanisms such as being accompanied by a special-needs classroom assistant, can also contribute to these processes. Further, the association of pupil learning difficulties with a notion of general intelligence, usually measured by some form of intelligence test, resulted in other labels for these types of children, such as 'slow learners', with the implication that their potential for learning was somehow fixed at birth. These essentialized views of capacity were to have profound consequences for many children after they left school.

Two strands of thinking can be identified: the first refers to a general incapacity and the second focuses on 'particular processing functions that are significantly discrepant in relation to an individual's other processing abilities. Some of these discrepancies have a profile with a label, such as: dyspraxia, dysgraphia and dyscalculia' (Reid, 2011: 153). This general incapacity can refer to problems relating to a pupil's organizational and synthesizing skills, compounded by deficiencies in a pupil's working memory – in short, a lack or deficit in their information processing skills. On the other hand, the particular diagnostic approach identifies, stigmatizes, and labels the child in relation to one of a set of specific learning difficulties. These might include:

> coordination difficulties; hyperlexia (low comprehension but good decoding skills); language and communication difficulties; dyslexia; auditory processing difficulties; hyperactivity; attention difficulties; dyscalculia; working-memory difficulties; information-processing difficulties; non-verbal difficulties; literacy difficulties; phonological processing difficulties; visual difficulties; social awareness difficulties.
>
> (Reid, 2011: 153)

Many of these specific learning difficulties can be placed on a continuum, and in addition, the existence of a specific learning difficulty does not preclude the existence of another one at the same time: for example, a pupil can be diagnosed with dyslexia and dyspraxia.

Definitions of these terms have proved controversial. There appears to be no agreed scientific basis for differentiating between someone who has been diagnosed as dyslexic, someone who has been diagnosed as a poor reader (this may of course refer to someone who is disinclined to learn), and a general reader. Dyslexia itself can be understood as a general portmanteau term to refer to almost any form of reading, decoding, and spelling difficulty. For example, the British Psychological Society suggests that '(d)yslexia is evident when accurate and fluent word reading and/or spelling develops very incompletely or with great difficulty. This focuses literacy learning at the word level and implies that the problem is severe and persistent despite appropriate learning opportunities' (British Psychological Society, 1999: 64). This all-embracing term, in its broad inclusivity, is then used in a vague and general way and consequently is not particularly useful for constructing remedial programmes. However, it may satisfy a need to know the condition that is afflicting someone, even if it doesn't in any way lead to an amelioration of the problem (with the problem being understood as a population norm, so that a comparison is being made with a notional idea of how that learner should be behaving).

Reiss and Brooks make this point in the following way:

> There are many definitions of dyslexia, but no consensus. Some definitions are purely descriptive while others embody causal theories. It appears that dyslexia is not one thing, but many, in so far as it serves as a conceptual clearing house for a number of reading skills, deficits and difficulties, with a number of causes. There is no consensus either, as to whether dyslexia can be distinguished in practice from other possible causes of adults' literacy difficulties. Many signs of dyslexia are no less characteristic of non-dyslexic people with reading skills deficits. In the present state of knowledge, it does not seem helpful for teachers to think of some literacy learners as 'dyslexics' and others as 'ordinary poor learners'.
>
> (Reiss and Brooks, 2004: 11)

Nevertheless, some organizations such as the British Dyslexia Association argue for a more precise definition, based on dyslexia as a neurological dysfunction:

> Dyslexia is a hidden disability [...] It is the most common of the SpLDs [...] A student with dyslexia may mix up letters within words and words within sentences while reading. They may also have difficulty with spelling words correctly while writing; letter reversals are common. However Dyslexia is not only about literacy, although weaknesses in literacy are often the most visible sign. Dyslexia affects the way information is processed, stored and retrieved, with problems of memory, speed of processing, time perception, organisation and sequencing. Some may also have difficulty navigating a route, left and right and compass directions.
>
> (British Dyslexia Association, n.d.)

We would expect this from an association formed with the purposes of identifying, treating, and eliminating a specific physiological condition, or at least one that is subscribing to a medical model of diagnosis, a behaviourist understanding of learning, and an essentialist and empiricist form of knowledge and knowledge-development (Scott, 2017).

The Salamanca Statement

The *Salamanca Statement and Framework for Action on Special Needs Education* (UNESCO, 1994) offered a new perspective on special needs education. In 1994 representatives of 92 national governments and 25 international organizations participated in the World Conference on Special Needs Education, in Salamanca, Spain, resulting in a statement about the principles underpinning inclusion in education. The Salamanca Statement endorsed the idea of inclusivity in educational institutions and thus the development of special needs education as an integral part of all educational programmes and policies. It sought to shift the focus from dis-ability as individual weakness and impairment to a strength, potential, and a function of arrangements in society. Difference was to be understood as normal, with the suggestion being that learning programmes should be adjusted to meeting needs rather than being 'fitted to preordained assumptions regarding the pace and nature of the learning process' (ibid.: 7).

The Salamanca Statement highlighted the importance of education for all children without at the same time establishing barriers to participation, such as through separate schools for the dis-abled and the abled. It also recommended a number of improvements in schools' structures, educational policies, and legislation, which would allow inclusive education to be realized. The principle of equality of opportunity for children with disabilities was recognized as a fundamental value and the suggestion was that it should inform all future and relevant legislation and policies. This meant that 'curricula should be adapted to children's needs, not vice-versa' (ibid.: 22), illustrating the importance of acknowledging individual interests and achievements. Educational support and relevant services offered to children with special educational needs, as well as teachers' and schools' preparedness in relation to special education, were recommended as appropriate measures in fostering inclusion.

The development of inclusive schools and the abolition of special schools, as far as possible, were the prime motivations behind the document:

> Regular schools which should accommodate them within a child-centered pedagogy capable of meeting these needs [...] regular schools with this inclusive orientation are the most effective

means of combating discriminatory attitudes, creating welcoming communities, building an inclusive society and achieving education for all; moreover, they provide an effective education to the majority of children and improve the efficiency and ultimately the cost-effectiveness of the entire education system.

(UNESCO, 1994, part 2: viii–ix)

The Salamanca Statement is a complex document full of conflicting arguments and unresolved tensions about inclusive education. It did, however, argue for inclusive policies and practices at the school, classroom, and individual levels, supplemented by appropriate forms of support.

These inclusive learning practices that formed the centrepiece of the document can be characterized through reconfigurations of learning environments: the simulation of the learning object, control in the pedagogic relationship, progression or its relations with other learning objects (i.e. curriculum integration), the type of pedagogic text, relations with other people in the learning process, the organization of time (temporal relations), and types of feedback mechanism. What this means is that in the learning process, the learning object takes on a new form as a result of changes to its properties: simulation, control, integration, textual form, relations with other people, time, and feedback. Though there is wide variation among inclusive schools there is a particular appropriation of all these issues.

The first of these is the degree and type of simulation. In a simulation a new medium is chosen which gives the learning object a new form. Indeed, depending on the new form, there is a distance between the original object and the mediated object, and this can vary in strength. Inevitably, the elements of the object and the relations between those elements are both reduced and changed in the simulation; what this means is that any reaction or response to the object by a learner is influenced by its new media, as well as the shape and form it now assumes. The response is always to the mediated object. And the implication of this is that the pedagogical relation between the learner and the world is never direct but is realized through the mediated object. An inclusive pedagogy has traditionally required the object of knowledge to have a strong mediated relationship.

A second property is control in the pedagogic relationship. Framing refers to the message system of pedagogy (Bernstein, 2000). Do teachers and pupils control its content, its organization, how it is sequenced, and so on? A syllabus with rigid topics, to be completed in a predetermined order, within a specified time, is strongly framed. Weak framing occurs when the teacher is able to select topics on the basis of some principle, and organize the sequence and pacing of material according to pupil readiness.

Two control pathways can be identified. The first refers to the relationship between the teacher and the learner on the one hand and, on the other, the curriculum organizers of knowledge (these organizing processes may be formal or informal), so a teacher or facilitator of the message system has either a restricted or extended control over the way it is received in the pedagogic setting. The second refers to the relationship between the teacher and the learner; again this refers to the amount of control either one or the other has over the constitution of the message that is central to the pedagogic or learning process. Clearly, in this last case the one varies in relation to variation in the other. The extent to which inclusive schools subscribe to weak or strong framings of the message system is an empirical matter, though in the past there has been evidence of strong framing regimes.

A third property is curriculum integration, or the types of relations between learning objects. Progression is one manifestation of these relations. Curriculum standards, or learning objects, are written at different levels of difficulty. Most forms of progression between levels or grades in national curricula around the world and in inclusive institutions are based on a notion of extension, that is, at Level 1 a student should be able to do this or that, at Level 2 the student is expected to be able to do more of this or that, and at Level 3 the student is expected to be able to do even more of this or that. However, there are other forms of progression between designated knowledge sets, skills, and dispositions besides extension, such as prior condition, maturation, intensification, and abstraction. Indeed, some knowledge sets, skills, and dispositions cannot be appropriately placed at some lower-level or even some higher-level grades.

Pace of learning is also important, that is, the pace at which a student works in completing a learning activity, or the pace at which they are expected to work against some norm, for example the average or mean of a population. Pace can be understood as a performative construct, so that it is not meant to provide an empirical description of how a person has performed but is designed to act as a stimulus to increase the pace of learning for the general population; it thus has an explicit normative function. And there is some evidence to suggest that some inclusive schools are resistant to performative notions of pace in the pedagogic relationship.

A fifth property is the constitution of the task given to the learner in the pedagogic setting. There is a range of learning tasks or activities that take place in classrooms, such as working with other people, individual study, sharing, debating, playing games, and so forth. Learning tasks have a number of constituent elements and how they differ in kind allows us to determine and identify these different elements: media of expression, the logic of this mediated expression, its fit with a learning model, its assessment mode, and its relation to real-life settings. Children who are statemented (i.e. who have a statement of special educational need) in mainstream schools have a different relationship to these elements. Exclusion can refer to institutional exclusion; however, it is more likely to refer to exclusion within an institution.

A sixth property is the relationship between the learner and other people in the pedagogic setting. One way of characterizing the relationship between the learner and the person, text, object in nature, particular array of resources, artefact, allocation of a role or function to a person, or sensory object is by determining its strength along a continuum ranging from a diffuse mode to a concentrated mode. This is a fundamental inclusive value. The key relationship for a statemented person in an inclusive school is with his or her special needs assistant.

Learning is always embedded in temporal arrangements of one kind or another. A curriculum is an arrangement of time given to different items of knowledge, so any learning episode is going to be embedded in these arrangements of time. There are feedback mechanisms and, again, there is variation in this element. Feedback is a systemic property (in the case we are considering here this is the learning process or system of inclusive education) and broadly consists of two types: feedback as it operates in closed systems and feedback as it operates in open systems. Closed systems are characterized by two conditions: objects operate in consistent ways, and they do not change their essential nature. Indeed, feedback mechanisms in this mode act to return the system to a state of equilibrium. Neither of these conditions pertains to open systems, which constitute most learning environments, inclusive or otherwise. If we consider these properties together – simulation, control, knowledge integration, textual form, relations with other people, time, and feedback – then it is possible to argue that it is the strength and extent of these properties in the practice that constitute the type of pedagogical approach that can be adopted and the types of learning that a child has in the inclusive school.

Inclusive educational policies in England

In England the first significant educational changes with regard to pupils with special educational needs in mainstream education were recommended in the Warnock Report of 1978. The Committee of Enquiry into the Education of Handicapped Children and Young People, chaired by Mary (later Baroness) Warnock, was appointed in November 1973 by the then secretary of state, Margaret Thatcher. Its remit was as follows:

to review educational provision in England, Scotland and Wales for children and young people handicapped by disabilities of body and mind, taking account of their needs, together with arrangements to prepare them for entry into employment; to consider the most effective use of resources for these purposes; and to make recommendations.

(Warnock, 1978: 1)

Its most important contribution was the recommendation that the term 'learning difficulties', rated as 'mild', 'moderate', and 'severe', be used, allowing these pupils to be included in mainstream educational schools and minimizing their social stigmatization (ibid.: 43). In the same report the term 'specific learning difficulties' was coined for the first time for those pupils who experience major difficulties in particular areas of learning, such as reading.

Some of the more important recommendations from the Warnock Report were as follows:

1. The planning of services for children and young people should be based on the assumption that about one in six children at any time and up to one in five children at some time during their school career will require some form of special educational provision (paragraph 3.17).
2. Statutory categorization of handicapped pupils should be abolished (paragraph 3.25).
3. The term 'children with learning difficulties' should be used in future to describe both those children who are currently categorized as educationally sub-normal and those with educational difficulties, who are often at present the concern of remedial services (paragraph 3.26).
4. In order to safeguard the interests of children with severe, complex, and long-term disabilities, there should be a system of recording as in need of special educational provision those children who, on the basis of a detailed profile of their needs prepared by a multi-professional team, are judged by their local education authority to require special educational provision not generally available in ordinary schools (paragraph 3.31).
5. Section 8(2)(c) of the Education Act 1944 and Section 5(1) of the Education (Scotland) Act 1962 (as amended), which define the duties of local education authorities in relation to the provision of special educational treatment and special education respectively, should be amended to embody a broader concept of special education related to a child's individual needs, as distinct from his or her disability, and a wider description of children which includes those with significant

difficulties in learning, or with emotional or behavioural disorders, as well as those with disabilities of mind or body (paragraph 3.42).

6. There should be five stages of assessment and a child's special needs should be assessed at one or more of these stages as appropriate (paragraph 4.35).

7. Where a district handicap team exists, it should be augmented as necessary so that it can carry out among its functions the assessment of children with special educational needs (paragraph 4.43).

8. The progress of a child with special educational needs should be reviewed at least annually and the head teacher of his school, whether an ordinary or a special school, should be responsible for initiating the review (paragraph 4.53).

9. The person who refers the child for multi-professional assessment should inform the parents as soon as the special education procedure is initiated and should give them a form on which to make their own statement about their child's needs (paragraph 4.60).

10. On the introduction of the new system, all children currently ascertained as requiring special educational treatment and also those who, though not so ascertained, are attending special schools or designated special classes or units should be recorded as requiring special educational provision (paragraph 4.71).

11. The education of children with disabilities or significant difficulties must start as early as possible without any minimum age limit. In the earliest years parents rather than teachers should be regarded, wherever possible, as the main educators of their children (paragraphs 5.2–5.3).

12. There should be a comprehensive peripatetic teaching service which would cater, wherever possible, exclusively for children with disabilities or significant difficulties below school age and cover every type of disability or disorder. There should be scope for specialization within the service; in particular, in view of the specific skills required for their teaching, children with sensory disabilities should be visited by teachers with related expertise (paragraph 5.37).

13. Nursery education provision for all children should be substantially increased as soon as possible, since this would have the consequence that opportunities for nursery education for young children with special needs could be correspondingly extended (paragraph 5.51).

14. Special nursery classes and units should be provided for young children with more severe or complex disabilities (paragraph 5.55).

15. Parents should be involved as closely as possible in the work of nursery schools and classes (paragraph 5.58).

16. The provision of combined day nurseries and nursery schools should be increased (paragraph 5.70).

17. More educational opportunities should be provided for children attending day nurseries, particularly those with special needs, and the staff should have opportunities to attend in-service courses organized on an inter-professional basis at which they would learn to recognize in children signs of special need and know when and where to refer for special help (paragraphs 5.69–5.71).

18. The lists of special schools published by the Department of Education and Science and the Scottish Education Department should, at least in the case of residential special schools, in future include details of the types of special educational need catered for (paragraph 6.14).

19. Each local education authority should produce and keep up to date a handbook containing details of special educational provision in its area for children recorded as requiring such provision. This handbook should include information about the types of special educational need catered for in individual schools as well as the names, office addresses, and telephone numbers of officers of the local education authority concerned with the provision of special education (paragraph 6.15).

20. Before a child with a disability or severe difficulty enters an ordinary school the teaching staff should discuss among themselves and agree a plan for securing the maximum educational and social interaction between him and others in the school, and should strive collectively thereafter to implement the plan (paragraph 7.21).

21. The head teacher should normally delegate day-to-day responsibility for making arrangements for children with special needs to a designated specialist teacher or head of department (paragraph 7.28).

22. Where one does not already exist, some form of resource centre or other supporting base should be established in large schools to promote the effectiveness of special educational provision (paragraph 7.32).

23. Where a resource centre, special class, or base is organized internally by the head teacher, the local education authority should arrange for the necessary staff and other resources to be made available to the school and should ensure that they are used for that purpose (paragraph 7.33).

24. Special classes and units should wherever possible be attached to and function as part of ordinary schools rather than be organized separately or attached to another kind of establishment such as a child guidance centre (paragraph 7.35).

25. Local education authorities should ensure that a school with a special class or unit is allotted an extra specialist teacher to its staffing complement (paragraph 7.36).

26. Children in special classes or units, whether attending full or part-time, should not form such a high proportion of the school roll or present such a range of needs as would substantially change the nature of the school (paragraph 7.38).

27. A variety of forms of short-term relief should be available for parents of children with severe disabilities who are living at home (paragraph 9.35).

28. Local education authorities should use their discretionary powers far more generously in making discretionary awards to students with disabilities or significant difficulties who enter further education (paragraph 10.16).

29. The teaching of child development in initial teacher training should always take account of different patterns and rates of individual development, particularly as they affect learning, and should include the effects of common disabilities and other factors which influence development (paragraph 12.6).

30. There should be a range of recognized qualifications in special education, to be obtained at the end of a one-year full-time course or its equivalent (paragraph 12.27).

31. All in-service courses designed for teachers who are specializing in the teaching of children with special educational needs should include consideration of working with parents and non-teaching assistants, peripatetic teaching and work with children below school age who require special help, as well as the principles of guidance and counselling (paragraph 12.36).

32. Every local education authority should restructure and, if necessary, supplement its existing advisory staff and resources to provide effective advice and support to teachers concerned with children with special educational needs through a unified service (paragraph 13.3).

33. A Special Education Research Group (SERG) should be set up with responsibility for indicating priorities for research in special education, for identifying programmes and projects to be initiated, for awarding some research grants, and for commenting if requested to do so on applications for research central to its concerns which are submitted to other research bodies. It should have at its disposal sufficient funds to enable it at any time to support one or two large programmes or projects, together with several smaller ones (paragraph 18.11).

34. Each local education authority should have a centre where research, development, and in-service training in special education are based and to which all the teachers in the area with responsibility for children with special needs can turn for help with their professional development (paragraph 18.17).

(adapted from Warnock, 1978)

Despite the lack of an agreed terminology of specific learning difficulties in the 1981 Education Act, which created confusions with regards to labelling, teaching strategies, and assessments for those pupils, that Act is viewed as a starting point for shifting the focus of English education from what pupils have to how pupils can be educated regardless of what they have. The 1993 Education Act and the 1994 Code of Practice, which followed, took these ideas further, and emphasized the significance of pupils' early identification and schools' provision for meeting their learning needs (DfE, 1994). Both terms 'specific learning difficulties' and 'dyslexia' were introduced at this time, and proponents suggested that dyslexia should be included among the specific learning difficulties, highlighting the schools' responsibility for pupils' identification, assessment, and learning support (DfE, 1994). Since then, a focused, targeted, highly structured and specified teaching programme based on pupils' previous performances and the nature of their difficulties was considered to be a suitable way of meeting those pupils' learning needs, enhancing their self-confidence and their academic success by using learning strategies to compensate for their difficulties.

However, the long process of pupils' early identification, which derived from parents' difficulties in convincing schools or local educational authorities of their children's difficulties, resulted in a loss of valuable time for effective interventions for those pupils, and had the effect of influencing in a negative fashion their progress, self-esteem, and confidence. In turn this situation highlighted the central importance of special educational needs statements for securing special provision. Acknowledging these weaknesses in the diagnostic process, a series of measures were recommended. These included early interventions by schools with well-structured assistance, as well as guidance being offered to trainee special educational needs coordinators (SENCO) on the nature and implications of specific learning difficulties for designing effective intervention programmes. Furthermore, differentiation in the teaching and assessment of pupils with specific learning difficulties was recommended, as they 'should not be expected to complete the same reading and writing tasks as other pupils of similar ability in the class, but should be provided with modified assignments which make allowances for their particular learning difficulties' (ibid.: 7). In practice, though, those pupils were examined with exactly the same assessment papers and the same assessment criteria as their peers.

Provision was made to allow the modification of national curriculum learning programmes in order to take into account pupils' abilities and to set learning challenges appropriate to their needs. Within that context, schools' interventions constituted a differentiation of materials and tasks. Similarly, the 2001 SEN Code of Practice underlined the importance of early identification of pupils' learning difficulties and of early intervention for ensuring their successful inclusion and full participation, allowing equal opportunities for all learners (DfES, 2001). However, the pressure to conform to a standards and accountability agenda has meant that schools generally follow the expected levels and developmental norms as they were promoted through the guidelines of the national curriculum.

Inclusive education has been an area of intense interest and focus since the publication of the Salamanca Statement. Such a multi-faceted and extensive concept of inclusion, though, needs to take into account the practical issues faced by schools when reconfiguring their educational programmes and structures to accord with inclusive principles. A reduction of emphasis on school accountability mechanisms and standardized performance levels has the potential to allow realistic expectations to be developed about children's learning and outcomes, and to improve the quality of education. The problematic implementation of inclusive education, though, poses more drawbacks for education, as it may negatively influence pupils' learning, progress, self-esteem, and socialization.

Pupils with special educational needs

The actual number of pupils with special educational needs fell from 1,301,445 in 2015 to 1,228,785 in 2016. This decline was caused by a continuing reduction in the number of special needs pupils without a statement or education, health and care (EHC) plan. In 2016, the latest available figures, 236,805 children had a statement or EHC plan. This amounted to 2.8 per cent of all pupils in full-time education. In total 991,980 pupils were receiving support for special educational needs. This constitutes 11.6 per cent of the total pupil population. Table 6.1 shows that the total number of pupils with special needs (statemented or receiving support) has remained stable, with some increase in the middle of this period, and a significant contraction at the end of it.

Table 6.1: Pupils with special educational needs, England, 2007–16

Year	Number of pupils with special needs
2007	1,632,000
2008	1,683,000
2009	1,702,000
2010	1,741,000
2011	1,728,000
2012	1,663,000
2013	1,502,000
2014	1,495,000
2015	1,301,000
2016	1,229,000

Source: DfE, 2016b: Table 1.

Official figures suggest that there is a range of types of special needs and subsequent proportions of each (see Table 6.2), though we have to be careful here to understand these types as provisional, developmental, historical, and as having power dimensions and dispositions.

Table 6.2: Pupils on SEN support or with a statement or EHC plan by type of need, England, 2016

	SEN support %	Statement or EHC plan %
Specific learning difficulties	15.6	4.0
Moderate learning difficulties	26.8	13.4
Severe learning difficulties	0.4	13.1
Profound and multiple learning difficulties	0.1	4.5
Social, emotional, and mental health needs	17.3	12.3
Speech, language, and communication needs	20.9	14.0
Hearing impairment	1.6	2.7
Visual impairment	0.9	1.5
Multisensory impairment	0.2	0.3
Physical disability	2.2	5.8
Autistic spectrum disorder	4.7	25.9
Other difficulty/disability	5.5	2.4

Note: pupils in state-funded primary, secondary, and special schools, England, 2016.

Source: DfE, 2016b: Table 8.

These pupils, or at least those with a statement or EHC plan, are unevenly distributed across the different types of schools, and this distribution has not changed to any great degree over the last seven years (see Table 6.3).

Table 6.3: Types of provision attended by pupils with a statement or EHC plan, England, 2010–16

School type	2010	2011	2012	2013	2014	2015	2016
Maintained nursery	0.1	0.1	0.1	0.1	0.1	0.1	0.1
State-funded primary	25.8	25.8	25.9	26.0	26.2	26.2	25.5
State-funded secondary	28.8	28.4	27.7	26.9	25.7	24.6	23.5
Maintained special	38.2	38.7	39.0	39.6	40.5	41.4	42.9
Pupil referral unit	0.9	0.8	0.7	0.7	0.7	0.7	0.6
Independent	4.2	4.3	4.7	4.9	5.1	5.3	5.7
Non-maintained special	2.0	1.9	1.9	1.8	1.7	1.6	1.6

Source: DfE, 2016b: Tables 1 and 2.

In 2016 special needs pupils were more likely to be boys than girls (see DfE, 2016b). Of the total male student population, 14.7 per cent were receiving special educational needs support, compared to 8.2 per cent of the total female population of students. Of the male population 4 per cent were statemented or had been given an EHC plan compared to 1.5 per cent of the female population (ibid.). Unsurprisingly, pupils with special educational needs were more likely to come from poorer families, as measured by the uptake of free school meals (ibid.). We need to distinguish here between eligibility for free school meals and take-up, because for a variety of reasons these are not the same. Given this proviso, 27.1 per cent of pupils with special educational needs were eligible for free school meals, compared with 12.1 per cent of pupils without educational needs. These figures, taken from Department for Education statistics (DfE, 2016b), show a closer correlation between the two categories than one would expect. Again, there may be a connection between ethnicity and having special needs status in schools, although we should be extremely careful about making these claims. (Members of a single ethnic group do not always share the same heritage stories.) However, travellers of Irish heritage and black Caribbean pupils tend to have slightly higher proportions of statements and EHC plans, and Indian pupils the lowest.

In the next chapter we examine inclusive and exclusive practices with regard to schooling. Before we do this, there is a need in relation to another of our categories to try to understand how sexualities are formed in societies and how practices of sexuality persist.

Sexuality

We close this chapter then with a brief look at sexuality, as the French philosopher, Michel Foucault, understood it (Foucault, 1988; 1990a; 1990b). Confessing sexual misconduct had long been an important part of the practice of religious confession, and while the Christian doctrine of the seventeenth and eighteenth centuries meant that these confessions were allowed to be less explicit, the range of what could be confessed also became much wider during these centuries. People were no longer just interested in confessing sexual deeds, but were also interested in confessing desires, thoughts, dreams; anything that could be associated with sex. Foucault contrasts this aspect of the Christian pastoral with the scandalous literature of later centuries that describes sex in exacting detail.

Thinking and writing about sex also extended far beyond the realm of the religious confessional. Sex became something to be studied rationally, to be analysed and classified, and understood as a statistical phenomenon. In the eighteenth century, people began to study demographics as a means of regulating the population. The sex lives of citizens became an important object of public scrutiny, as statistics regarding birth rates, fertility rates, illegitimate births, and so on became important for public use. This scrutiny took a particular form. Foucault (1979: 184) suggests that the examination of sexuality 'combines the techniques of an observing hierarchy and those of a normalizing judgment'. (He was writing about the technique of examination at the time, but the remark applies equally to sexuality.) Further to this, '(i)t is a normalizing gaze, a surveillance that makes it possible to qualify, to classify and to punish [and i]t establishes over individuals a visibility through which one differentiates them and judges them' (ibid.). This normalizing gaze enables society to construct individuals as sexual beings. Knowledge of persons is created, which has the effect of binding individuals to each other, embedding those individuals in networks of power, and sustaining mechanisms of surveillance, which are all the more powerful because they work by allowing individuals to govern themselves. This introduces a whole new mechanism that both contributes to a new type of knowledge formation about sex and constructs a new network of power, which is all the more persuasive once it becomes established throughout society.

This mechanism works in three ways: first, by transforming 'the economy of visibility into the exercise of power' (ibid.: 187); second, by introducing 'individuality into the field of documentation' (ibid.: 189); and third, by making 'each individual a case' (ibid.: 191). In the first instance, power is exercised invisibly: this contrasts with the way power networks in the past operated visibly, through the explicit exercise of force. This invisibility works by imposing on subjects a notion of objectivity that acts to bind them to a truth about their sexuality, a truth that is hard to resist, and by 'arranging objects' (ibid.: 187) or people in particular ways in society. In the second instance, the mechanism allows the individual to be archived by being inscribed textually. People are increasingly subject to disciplinary regimes of individual measurement and assessment concerning their sexuality, which have the further effect of determining them as cases.

The third of Foucault's modalities refers to the objectification of the individual as a branch of knowledge, so that the individual could be described, judged, measured, and compared with others, and never more so than in relation to their sexuality and its formation (in pedagogic settings). One final point needs to be made about this objectification, and this is that for the first time the individual could be scientifically categorized and characterized through a modality of power where difference becomes the most important factor. Hierarchical normalization becomes the dominant way of organizing society. Foucault is suggesting here that the treatment of sex as a statistical phenomenon, on the surface a neutral activity, acts to position the person being examined in a discourse of normality, so that for them to understand themselves in any other way is to understand themselves as abnormal and even as unnatural. This positioning works to close off the possibility of the person understanding themself in any other way, though it may not be successful.

Foucault argues that sexuality in the nineteenth century was in its essentials repressive. Consequently, sex was treated as a private affair, which was rarely talked about except in an excessively prurient way, and was generally confined to marital relations. Sex outside these parameters was repressed, and may even have been prohibited. Here, there was an attempt not just to prevent sex outside marriage but also to make it unthinkable, to reconfigure it so that it was not talked about as a wholesome pleasure. This repressive hypothesis also suggests that there are particular outlets of confession, where sexual feelings can be safely assuaged, such as in prostitution and psychiatry. The twentieth century was no different. Sigmund Freud may have permitted open and frank discussions of sexuality, but such talk was still confined to the academic and confessional realms of psychiatry. Foucault suggests that, starting with the rise of the bourgeoisie in the seventeenth century, tighter controls were placed on how we could talk and write about sex. In other words, there were efforts made to control sex at the level of speech, although they rarely worked.

While discourses on sex had previously dealt solely with marriage, that is, what one was allowed to do and what one was prohibited from doing, they came increasingly to focus on those who fell outside the category of marriage: children, homosexuals, the mentally ill, and so on. A distinction was created between legal violations of marriage bonds and natural violations, with the latter being seen as sick or demented. Since the eighteenth century, efforts have been made to identify and classify non-marital sexual practices.

Foucault identifies four activities that extend the notion of sexual perversion. The first of these takes us beyond the notion of repression with regard to studying child sexuality. Foucault is more concerned with a general examination of sexuality, and contends that it is as the result of examination per se that strong and impermeable boundaries are established between adult sexuality and child sexuality. Children are excluded from the realm of sexuality, with an attempt being made to desexualize children; however, this has the perverse consequence that, instead of restricting what might constitute a discourse about sexuality, it has the effect of extending it to a number of different areas, such as gendered relations, legal prohibitions, and the like.

The second activity is identity formation: this considers how, for example, the modern concept of homosexuality now goes much deeper than in earlier understandings and is held as a fundamental part of our being. Before the nineteenth century, 'sodomy' was quite simply understood as a criminal act, and nothing more. Over time homosexuality ceased being just a behaviour or act, and was now understood, existentially, as the base or core of the person. This meant that the sexuality of the person became the key to interpreting what that person was. Rather than striving to eliminate homosexual acts, the growing discourse surrounding homosexuality saw these acts as central to and constitutive of a person's identity.

A third element focuses on what Foucault calls 'spirals of power and pleasure'. The much closer scrutiny that is an essential part of the medicalization of sexuality draws the investigator and the person being investigated together, much more intimately. On the one hand, the investigator exercises power through their examination of another person's sexual pleasures, and this exercise of power may give them a vicarious sense of pleasure. On the other hand, in the investigative act, the subject of this investigation may also experience pleasure. Both the investigator and the person being investigated find power and pleasure in this intimate game of examination.

Furthermore, this confessional act is seen as therapeutic. In the twentieth century, psychiatrists and psychoanalysts tried to turn the intimate confession of the person being investigated into a scientific discourse, or, as Foucault calls it, a confessional science of sex. He suggests that this amalgamation of confession and science works in five ways. The first of these is through the adoption of specific methods, such as examination, free association, and even hypnosis; these were designed to regulate the process of extracting a confession. Secondly, by widening the purview of sexuality and understanding it as a possible cause of a variety of different behaviours, a more precise and exact form of confession was formulated. Thirdly, sexuality was now understood as latent and concealed, which demanded the invention of methods that would bring it to the surface. Fourthly, the psychoanalytical process embraced a notion of confessional dialogue between the investigator and the person being investigated. And finally, perceiving confession as therapeutic gave it the ambience of a medical procedure.

What this meant was that the tradition of the confessional was being combined with a scientific discourse, and this contributed to our modern notion of sexuality. Consequently, sexuality is not properly understood if all we do is treat it as a repressive mechanism. What we need to do is understand it as a socially constructed form of power relations. Our modern concept of sexuality serves as a network that joins together physical sensations and pleasure, the formation of specialized knowledge, and political forms of resistance.

This relation of sex to power and knowledge, then, is Foucault's principal contribution to understanding sexuality, and it works in a number of ways. The first of these is through the 'hysterization of women's bodies' (Foucault, 1990a: 34), so that women's bodies are both seen as highly sexual and as objects of medical knowledge. In addition, the female body and its reproductive capacity are now considered matters of public interest and public control. The second of these is the 'pedagogization of children's sex' (ibid.), in which children are understood as highly sexualized beings, and this sexuality is then thought of as dangerous and therefore needing to be monitored and controlled. Thirdly, the 'socialization of procreative behaviour' (ibid.) understands sex and reproduction as matters of public interest, and combines this with a disapproval of non-procreative sex. Finally, the 'psychiatrization of perverse pleasure' (ibid.) results in the study of sex as being a medical and psychiatric phenomenon. These four mechanisms contribute in combination to the formation of an idea of normality, or a sexual norm, which in effect has the power to pathologize sexual behaviour, so that anything that diverges from normal sexual behaviour can be identified as an illness or pathology that needs correcting. At the time of writing this book, ministers in the UK have announced compulsory sex and relationships education throughout the national curriculum, and more controversially, for four-year-olds. The programmes of study are to include consent, sexting, and online grooming. From this discussion of discourses (i.e. dis-ability and sexuality), we move to an examination of practices, and specifically, inclusive and exclusive practices.

Chapter 7

Inclusion and exclusion: Educational practices

We have attempted in this book to show how powerful discourses work in relation to six important striations in the social landscape: gender, race, dis-ability, intelligence, sexuality, and class. In this chapter we focus on inclusive and exclusive practices in education. We have suggested that a discourse is a set of propositions about the world, joined together by a set of connectives and relations, that offers an account of an object or objects in the world, and may even act to create objects in the world. However, what needs to be said repeatedly is that a discursive construction can never be a simple determinant of identity, behaviour, or action. Discourses, then, are structured in a variety of ways, and both this meta-structuring and the forms it produces are relative to time and place. These meta-forms refer to issues such as generality, performativity, reference, value, binary opposition, representation, and legitimacy.

We also need to make sense of the notion of change or alteration. Objects and relations between objects change their form over time. An example of this change process at the epistemological level is the invention (in so far as the set of concepts and relations between them is new) of the notion of probability (Hacking, 1990) in the nineteenth century, which changed the way social objects could be conceived and ultimately arranged. Change can occur in four ways: contingent ontological, planned ontological, epistemically driven ontological, and, in the transitive realm of knowledge, epistemological (Scott, 2011). With regard to the example above, the invention of probability, two phases of change can be identified. The first is where knowledge is created and thus operates at the epistemological level, the new arrangement of knowledge. The second is where this knowledge has real effects at the ontological level, so that new arrangements, new formations, new assemblages come into being. The dilemma is that the social world, in contrast to the physical world, is always in a state of transition and flux, so that it is hard to argue that there are invariant laws by which the world works, at all times and in all places, except in a basic logical and rational sense.

Society is characterized by notions of continuous emergence, flux, and change. Objects in the world cannot be characterized by their essential qualities, but only through their interactions with other objects. Complexity resides in all these various interactions, which produce new objects (characterized as different forms of structure) and result in a bewildering array of arrangements of material and human objects. Because they are difficult to characterize they rarely allow definitive accounts of what is going on to be produced. It is the complexity of these object-interactions and their subsequent and temporary coalescences that makes it difficult to provide complete descriptions of them. The epistemic level is unsynchronized with the ontic level, because researchers and investigators have not developed sufficiently their instruments and conceptual schema for capturing something that is both ever-changing and has too many elements to it – that is, the ontic level is too complex. However, this doesn't categorically rule out the possibility of providing more complete descriptions of events, structures, mechanisms, and their relations in the world, and this suggests a notion of human fallibility, which means that our actions are corrigible. The twin elements of complexity and temporal emergence cannot preclude correct descriptions being made of activities in the world; the situation only entails that these elements can create considerable difficulties. This is further compounded by how emergence operates in the world.

Many theorists go further than this (e.g. Osberg and Biesta, 2007), and hold to a version of emergence in which there is a radical incommensurability between different formations over time (whether material, embodied, or discursive). Furthermore, they argue, it is impossible to predict what inter-connections, new formations, and iterations of the object-system will be realized, because the principles of the new mechanism are not given in the current arrangements. In other words, the relations between objects and the objects themselves that make up activity systems are not patterned in any meaningful sense; there is a radical incommensurability between these different iterations.

All discussions of a person over time require some understanding of change; that is, the notion of change is built into the conception of the human being. There is also the problem of persistence. If there was no cohering element between time moments, so that every moment entails a change of person, we would not have a sense of personhood – which therefore also has to include a notion of *persistence* over time, and in addition has a notion of *emergence*. And this is emergence understood in its two modes: as a temporal phenomenon and ontologically as a response to the stratified nature of reality.

We are dealing here with change and the various ways it can be understood. The most common form of organized change, much used by governments, is confiscation. If a person is denied a good (through confiscation of money, such as being fined, or other goods, or being prevented from realizing an opportunity to acquire a good) then their condition of equality, relative to other persons or previous states they were in, has changed. They have become less equal, with regard to goods, opportunities, and life conditions. A different, but equally powerful, change mechanism is where the conditions for the instantiation of the categories (i.e. values relating to generality, performativity, reference, valuation, binary opposition, representation, and legitimacy) are altered. This operates at the epistemological level but it may have ontological consequences.

Inclusive education

One of the most important change mechanisms is directly political. We have referred in great detail to mechanisms of this type with regard to the English education system, and in particular to private education (see Chapter 2), teacher training (Chapter 3), selection and de-selection in the public education system (Chapter 4), examination and testing (Chapter 5), and special needs education (Chapter 6). Three models of the policy process can be formulated. The first is a centrally directed policy process. Policy makers given a democratic mandate construct a set of policy recommendations, which are then put out for consultation. After they have considered the points made in response, they write orders and implement the policy prescriptions of those who have been elected to office. The process is one-way, directive, and, depending on the intentions and motivations of the policy makers, designed to support a particular set of values.

The second model is pluralist, where a variety of interests are taken into consideration at every stage of the policy process: these stages are policy making, policy presentation, and policy implementation. Policy itself is represented as a continuous process of the making and remaking of the original intentions of the policy maker. The process is multifaceted and pluralist; indeed, the policy text cannot be said to be authored as such, because it is the combined work of a large number of people operating at different levels of the system and at different sites. However, it has democratic legitimacy, as a variety of interested parties are involved in its construction. These interests are identified and their representations are considered and incorporated into the policy process itself. The relay between policy making and policy implementation is unilinear, though this model comprises a more sophisticated understanding of the way policy is constructed.

A number of problems with this model have been identified. The first of these is that the model separates out policy making from policy implementation. The thrust of the argument is that policies are made and then implemented and these two processes are understood as distinct but sequentially related activities. The second objection to this model is that it fails to identify the unequal way different interests are identified and represented at the initial stages of policy making. For example, it fails to recognize the power of the central authority to impose its will, not by acting to exclude representations of the various competing parties that have an interest in the activities being considered, but by manipulating the process so that only those interests that the central authority considers to be closely aligned with their own preferred way of understanding are allowed to influence the process. This can be achieved relatively easily. For example, the central authority can control appointments to the various advisory bodies which are set up to feed into the policy making process the views of a diverse range of interested parties: this control mechanism is used to eliminate and marginalize some views and foreground others. Furthermore the central authority can control the agenda for discussion, thus excluding some views and promoting others. Thirdly, this view of policy suggests that policy makers always have a clear idea of what they want and how it can be achieved. It therefore ignores the serendipitous and muddled nature of the policy process.

If we are to develop this model of how policy works, we need to take account of the type of flow or relay between the various constituent parts of the process, how powerful people can manipulate the process, and the unforeseen consequences of decisions made by policy makers because they do not understand or do not have the foresight to imagine what will happen to their policy prescriptions during implementation. Three forms of implementation may occur: adaptive extension of the original policy, accommodation of the new proposals with the consequence that they may not have a decisive or radical impact, and containment, where the policy is absorbed into the existing routines of the recipient body and therefore to some extent marginalized.

We have referred in this book to the radical changes made by successive UK governments to the structures of education in England, such as introducing a national curriculum and a national assessment system. These policy prescriptions can then be adaptively extended, accommodated, or contained. Governments, in turn, have responded to these blocking devices in a number of ways. The first is to write policy documents and directives so that they are more prescriptive and less open to interpretation; in other words, they close off opportunities for practitioners to resist the intentions behind government policies. The second response is to direct their attention to reallocating control within the system, so that recontextualizing bodies that act as forms of resistance are stripped of powers. We can see this most clearly in the demise over the last twenty years of the local education authorities (LEAs). The third response is to create new regulatory bodies, such as the Office for Standards in Education (Ofsted), which has the power and resources to compel schools through inspection to change their practice if it does not conform to what is expected by government. Finally, changing the financial settlement between the different parts of the system (and in particular reallocating the control of funds to different players and organizations within the system) is another way of initiating change.

In a third model policy is always understood as existing in a state of flux, as policy texts are continually interpreted and reinterpreted at every point in the relay. Furthermore, powerful actors at the various sites of influence respond to what they consider to be the unintended consequences of the implementation of their policies and in the process rewrite or reconfigure both their policies and the means of their implementation. This they never fully achieve, because the policy setting is always so complex that policy makers, however hard they try, are never in a position to control events. In addition, they frequently operate with misunderstandings of the policy process and faulty information about the effects of their policies. This is because the political process demands that they justify their actions to various scrutinizing bodies and the means for doing this are rarely in their control.

Each of the policy sites has its own set of rules about how truth is constructed. Actors at each of these sites may or may not be aware of this, and indeed in following the rules change and amend them in various ways. Furthermore, those different sets of rules at the various sites are frequently in conflict, so, for example, the actual rules that underpin media reporting of educational issues are at odds with the site of implementation, that is, the schools. This of course contributes to the fragmentation of the policy process. However, we should not underestimate the way in which individual policy actors are more or less powerful in relation to each other, and that more powerful actors can exert pressure in various ways on those that are less powerful. One way of doing this is to position the reader of influential policy texts within a binary divide of normality/abnormality as to how they think and act.

Understanding diversity and exclusion

We now need to explore the implications of recent education policy developments for inclusive education in England and also in other parts of the world. We are doing this in order to suggest possibilities and the means to change the system from one form to another. Given that globalizing education policy expresses an ethic of competitive individualism (see Rizvi and Lingard, 2010), our concern here is with issues of diversity and exclusion in a globalizing education context, and from this we suggest that a framework for inclusive education can be developed. This framework for inclusion is built from particular understandings of governance and accountability arrangements, professionalism and resilience, localized reforms, and relationships between learning opportunities and the community.

Such an exploration allows us to identify important elements of inclusive education. Any framework for inclusion is founded upon a comprehensive understanding of the local context and the specific dynamics of inclusion and exclusion. This discussion draws on international literature to provide examples of dismantling barriers to educational access, participation, and success. Reflecting on the OECD review of education for migrant and disadvantaged populations (OECD, 2010a) in various social contexts enables us to examine contested policy approaches and consider approaches to inclusion across a range of educational and cultural contexts. Central to the aspirations of reform is an adherence to the principles of inclusion and justice. Consequently, community and family engagement are at the heart of reforming education. Here we suggest ways of developing more inclusive educational and social responses to exclusion.

Inclusive education is broadly 'understood as a reform that supports and welcomes diversity amongst all learners' (UNESCO, 2009: 8). The diversity of learners and thus their differences is understood in a broad sense within the inclusive education discourse: it refers to such matters as ability or dis-ability, ethnic origin, religion, sexual orientation, race, gender, and economic class. Further to this, inclusive education points to an amelioration or betterment of the effects of discrimination by the school and the whole society, directed towards accepting, representing, and celebrating differences. This also caters for and addresses the individual needs of students in order to tackle their educational as well as their social exclusion. The transformation of the (inclusive) school is understood as a constant process within the inclusive education discourse.

It is important to understand that the discourse of inclusive education is not always a reliable indicator of inclusive educational practice. Education jurisdictions around the world have readily adopted the language of inclusion while maintaining assumptions about the nature of student differences and academic achievement that maintain the educational architecture of exclusion. Inclusive education has become an important priority for both political and educational systems worldwide. Inclusive education draws on a number of old and well-established social and political values, such as safeguarding and promoting social inclusion, equal opportunities, human rights, social justice, social respect, participation, achievement, diversity, and solidarity (UNESCO, 2009). Furthermore, it is legitimized through a number of legal frameworks, both older and well established as well as more recent ones, including the 1979 Convention on the Elimination of All Forms of Discrimination Against Women, the 1989 Convention on the Rights of the Child, the 2005 Convention on the Protection and Promotion of the Diversity of Cultural Expressions, and the 2006 Convention on the Rights of Persons with Disabilities. These international conventions are instantiated in local anti-discrimination and equal opportunity legislation.

As we saw in Chapter 6, during the 1970s the influential Warnock Report in the UK (Warnock, 1978) described the placing of 'children with special needs' in segregated schools as an exclusionary practice. Further to this, the report emphasized the urgent need for children to be integrated into mainstream schools in order to overcome their physical marginalization by placing them alongside their peers and by offering them a special educational needs (SEN) programme. From this standpoint, integration came to be opposed to the notion of segregation. However, the integration agenda has been criticized for disregarding the differences between people and for assuming that children should be acculturated and assimilated into an already existing, stable, and fixed educational system.

Inclusive reform agendas

Reform agendas, however well intentioned, have the potential to either attenuate or exacerbate social disparities and exclusions. Schools, research tells us, are powerful agents of social exclusion (Wilkinson and Pickett, 2009), and this research is long-standing and extensive. The development of what was then called the 'new sociology of education' (e.g. Bowles and Gintis, 1976) investigated the ways in which the school curriculum was founded upon and reinforced the cultural attributes of children from class elites (Bourdieu and Passeron, 1977). As a result, children from privileged families successfully completed school and their transition into higher education and professional work was typically seamless. This was not the case for working-class children, who were failed by school. They left school before completing their education and found their place in the semi-skilled and unskilled labour market. Immigrant children, indigenous children, children living in isolated communities, and disabled children are amongst those who have also experienced forms of educational exclusion. Sadly, this research has not been made redundant by history. League tables and high-stakes testing programmes around the world have in addition had the effect of inducing schools to exclude students whose educational prospects looked to be weak and who would therefore have negative effects on school inspection reports and league table positions.

An example of a more inclusive education policy is the Finnish system. As a result of its strong welfare state, which supports the education system and economic stability, public education is provided free as a universal and constitutional right. Finnish schools are considered as focal centres for their communities. Regardless of students' social class, schools provide the necessary resources and free hot meals, as well as health and dental services, psychological counselling, and a broad array of other services for students and their families.

A low student-to-teacher ratio enables teachers to maximize the learning opportunities for their students, with greater opportunities for teachers to give their students individual attention. The Finnish approach to students with difficulties is early detection and intervention, rather than problem solving and individual support. With the assistance of a 'special teacher', students who need extra assistance are identified and receive individual assistance based on learning plans developed for individual needs (OECD, 2011). Every comprehensive school in Finland has a pupils' multi-professional care group, consisting of the principal, the special education teacher, the school nurse, the school psychologist, a social worker, the teachers whose students are being discussed, and the parents (where this is considered to be appropriate). The group meets at least every other week to discuss the classroom situation in general and particular students who face difficulties, and to decide on appropriate supports to be put in place. It is estimated that nearly two out of five students in Finnish schools have received part-time and full-time special interventions by the time they finish comprehensive school, which means that, in such an environment, special education is not considered 'special'.

In Finland, teachers spend less time teaching in lower secondary education compared to the average for OECD countries (OECD, 2010b). However, teachers commit much of their extra time to activities outside the classroom, including supporting students with special needs. More time is also invested in professional learning and applications to improve the school as a whole, and to improve classroom practice and work with the community.

Research on reform initiatives in inclusive education reveals the inextricable link between historically ingrained social inequality and educational exclusion (e.g. Ainscow, 2016). This is manifested in the quality and quantity of life opportunities in education, healthcare, housing, employment, and various forms of social participation. Canada, for example, ranks highly in literacy levels measured on test scores as well as in economic prosperity, but has been associated with poor performance in the areas of health and safety, family and peer relations, and subjective wellbeing (UNICEF, 2007). A mismatch between the levels of national wealth measured in GDP per capita and overall child wellbeing, including education and even material wellbeing, is also evident among some of the OECD nations; the United States, the UK, Austria, and France are seen to rank lower in these regards compared to poorer nations such as the Czech Republic (Wilkinson and Pickett, 2009). In the state of California, Slee (2010) suggests that low educational achievement in schools is due to poor nutrition and health among disadvantaged children, which may have the effect of reducing concentration, school attendance, and academic achievement. Slee further suggests that governments and researchers often portray the issue of poverty as 'pathological', rather than seeing it as socially constructed. It is treated as a political fact, rather than as 'an outcome of particular political, economic and social relations' (ibid.: 2). The implication of this is that the improvement of the quality of life for disadvantaged students can be enhanced by eschewing the reduction of education to human capital production through test-score performance and by building social and community capital through focusing on local settings.

The success or otherwise of inclusive education practices hinges on the development of system-wide approaches to redefine desirable skills and qualities in education, and on being able to communicate these across diverse community contexts while simultaneously building on individual school and community developments through networked local initiatives. Exclusive approaches and assumptions in policy reforms are considered to be barriers to the successful implementation of inclusion policies. For example, it has been suggested that the following approaches have resulted in ineffective policy reforms in England: policy being exclusively targeted at disadvantaged, low-attaining groups without taking into consideration the complex of inter-linked factors that attribute to their positions, such as socio-economic arrangements in society and differences interpolated in language structures; the prioritizing of structural reforms by adopting single-issue responses rather than holistic interventions; and valuing a limited range of measured attainments over and against the full range of educational purposes.

Dyson *et al.* suggest that politicians continue to propose 'solutions' under the assumption that the problem of inequality can be solved when they find 'a right combination of interventions and structural arrangements' (Dyson *et al.*, 2010: 27). They warn us that this approach of targeting failing schools and underachieving groups will continue to fail so long as initiatives are 'overlaid on […] an inherently unfair system' and are 'compounded by the competitive, standards-driven nature of the system itself' (ibid.). Wilkinson and Pickett (2009), in their survey of affluent countries, surmise that, as a result, where inequality is high the country will rate at a lower level across a range of social indicators, including education.

A framework for inclusive education

To create a more equitable education system through reform, Dyson *et al.* (2010) suggest three major and overlapping areas of concern: localization, creating suitable learning opportunities, and establishing strong governance and accountability arrangements. In pursuit of this agenda, an emphasis on the local area is foregrounded. This helps stakeholders understand and respond to the presence of, and dynamic relationships between, social and cultural identities in the area, local needs, interests, and resources, as well as the way education and relevant opportunities, public and private activities, are linked and coordinated. This analysis focuses on identifying these social, cultural, economic, and political factors and the complex ways in which educational inequalities are created, so that the best strategies can be developed.

Creating suitable learning opportunities is a part of providing 'learning opportunities for community engagement and development' (Dyson *et al.*, 2010: 9). Dyson *et al.* suggest that in order to achieve greater equity across an education system, the curriculum, scope, and opportunities for education need to reflect the characteristics of the locality, and stakeholders need access to diverse pathways that suit available employment and other future pathways and options for young people in the area. The identification and creation of such learning opportunities and future pathways require the involvement of the whole community, including the family and local industry.

Governance and accountability arrangements address the issue of gathering data useful for teaching and learning that increase teachers' professional capacity and ownership of the process, in contrast to currently existing accountability regimes that have diverted practitioners' attention away from important elements of reform and teaching. Finally, to enable such concerns to be implemented in order to accomplish inclusive education projects, the model suggests that high levels of professionalism and resilience need to be generated by the reform authority with all the stakeholders, including teachers, school staff and leaders, community workers, policy makers, and other relevant professionals.

Another example of a successful inclusion initiative is the most recent Index for Inclusion (Booth and Ainscow, 2011). This is an excellent resource for education systems seeking to reduce exclusion and build sustainable forms of inclusive schooling. Here, inclusive education is represented as an agent for providing fair and appropriate educational opportunities for disabled and disadvantaged children. The Index for Inclusion provides strategies for creating inclusive cultures, producing inclusive policies, and evolving inclusive practices in the school. The focus is upon bringing the school community together to interrogate the nature and impacts of their school's culture, policies, and practices.

Inclusive policies can be encouraged by changing the financial arrangements in the system. In 1995, the New Zealand government introduced Targeted Funding for Educational Achievement (TFEA) as a component of the schools' operating grants. TFEA is targeted to assist schools to overcome barriers to students' achievement that are associated with socio-economic disadvantage. TFEA is not tied to any particular school activity. In 1998, the value of grants provided to schools through TFEA was approximately NZ$50 million, just over 7 per cent of the NZ$676 million committed to overall operating grants in that year. Using the TFEA indicator, every state and state-integrated school is ranked according to the presence of students from low socio-economic status communities to determine funding allocations. Schools are subdivided into 10 deciles and lower deciles comprise schools with greater funding needs. Per-student funding is graduated; it increases as the school's decile declines. TFEA funding is allocated to decile 1–9 schools. According to the rate in 2010, per-student funding ranged from NZ$819.75 for a decile 1A school to $26.18 for a decile 9 school (Ministry of Education, New Zealand, 2011).

Edge (2001: 8) explains that the TFEA socio-economic indicator is calculated using a census mesh-block (a small geographic area) and school ethnicity data. It takes into account household income, parents' occupation and educational qualifications, household crowding, parents' income support payments, and Maori and Pacific Peoples' ethnicity. The rating is reviewed automatically every five years and can also be reviewed once per year if schools believe their socio-economic status make-up has changed significantly (e.g. because of a plant shutdown). Clearly, changes to the financial arrangements between central authorities and their schools have the potential to impact on the system in other ways, and in particular to affect inclusive school initiatives.

Over the last two centuries, industrialization and the expansion of public education have opened access to education to wider sections of society, including women, indigenous children, and disabled children. However, the transformation of schooling to mass education has forged education system hierarchies. Recent trends such as globalization, standardization, and market-driven educational reforms have favoured high-stakes testing and accountability regimes that have contributed to a widening of the school–community gap. With broader societal challenges for schooling, the nature of teachers' work has become increasingly complex and demanding. With increasingly diversified societies and a new educational landscape, the involvement of communities in education is an important factor in educational success. Because of this, teacher training and the structure of schools need to consider the contributions of new partners within the community. Through systemic reform, diverse institutions and stakeholders may be required to establish their complementary roles to make the reform initiative sustainable.

Inclusive education policies

In this chapter we have explored the implications of recent education policy developments for inclusive education in England and in other parts of the world. We have discussed current notions of diversity and exclusion in a globalizing education context, and then proposed a framework for inclusive education. The focus here has been on productive practices relating to the removal of barriers to inclusive education. In some jurisdictions inclusive education merely describes education policies and practices for dis-abled (in both a physical and learning sense) students. We have taken a broader view of inclusive education as a response to all forms of educational exclusion. Inclusive education therefore refers to the dismantling of barriers to education for all students.

Inclusive education proceeds from an informed understanding of diversity and exclusion. Schools and school systems have always been powerful agents of exclusion. School organization, the content of the curriculum and the values it expresses, the preferred form of teaching and learning, and assessment methods combine to reinforce social elitism. This is true for many societies, developed or developing.

Many recent reforms to schooling have contributed to the exclusion of vulnerable children. Vulnerability may be associated with race, religious affiliation, poverty, disability, geographic isolation, gender, or refugee status. Ranking schools on the basis of students' performance on tests encourages schools to be more selective. As we have suggested here, these practices have a deleterious effect upon minority groups and economically disadvantaged students. This is not a rejection of standards; rather it is a call for more inclusive pedagogical practices to support all students' access to and participation and success in schooling.

The model of inclusion we favour here supports the view that increasing segregated special education provision for students with disabilities is not inclusive education. Committing scarce resources to a bifurcated system is wasteful. Lessons from jurisdictions such as Finland support the findings of Wilkinson and Pickett's (2009) study of inequality and social and economic wellbeing that aims to address inequality in schooling and other social institutions, and support the aspirations and strategies of inclusive education. Moreover, we suggest that a more inclusive approach to schooling can result in an overall improvement in students' achievement levels.

Developing more inclusive education that addresses the disadvantages experienced by children in scheduled tribes and castes, the girl child, disabled children, and traveller and displaced children is achieved through teacher and community education as well as reforms to education policy. It is also important to attend to the curriculum as a key strategy to build more inclusive schooling. Evidence from the UK, Australia, Canada, and New Zealand shows that when minority students are exposed to a curriculum that acknowledges their identity, they become more engaged with learning.

The English education system

Technical-rationality thinking makes the assumption that change can be predicted or at least can be read off from the presumed effects of causal mechanisms. These causal mechanisms then presuppose that if a set of common elements are present and combine together appropriately, this will result in a standardized result. The understanding is that any set of causal mechanisms operates in a linear and predictable pattern and effects can thus be read off from causes that persist across time. As a result educational systems are relatively stable, though within such systems there are mechanisms for improvement, such as meeting the needs of accountability and incentivization processes. Complex systems thinking is premised on the idea that systems do not change in this simple way but are non-linear, unpredictable, and in effect at a meta-level cannot be described. This is chaos theory, not in the sense that one should despair of ever being able to describe, predict, and propose change to control the system, but that the system is in truth complex. To reduce it to a set of demands for control by policy makers is to do it a disservice. We have a responsibility to try to understand it as it is. The logic of targets and standards (a typical reform mechanism) therefore only makes sense if one adopts an uncomplicated and non-complex view of the way a system operates. The need to build into our theory the non-predictability of reading off what is going to happen within a system is as a result essential.

It is possible to trace some of the developments in and changes to the forms of educational governance in England, concentrating on the largest part of the UK as we have done. This is not a complete history of educational reform in England, since the volume of centrally directed experiments and interventions has been such that it is difficult to document them all. However, this period can be characterized as one of continuous change, flux, and perturbation, in which successive governments experimented with, intervened in, and changed the governance of the system. Changing the types of rewards and sanctions for teachers, the criteria for judging quality within the system, the compliance capacity of the workforce, and how they judged themselves and each other, contributed to changing the learning experiences of children. Ball (2008) argues that the processes of public sector transformation in the English education system had five key elements: de-concentration, disarticulation and diversification, flexibilization, destatization, and centralization. The first of these, he suggests, was the 'devolving of budgets and teacher employment to the school level' (ibid.: 24). The second of these processes, that of disarticulation and diversification, refers to processes such as the weakening of the local government structure, the introduction of new types of schools with different governance and financing arrangements (e.g. city technology colleges, grant-maintained schools, academies, and free schools), and diversification, so that, as Ball suggests, there is 'a self-conscious attempt to promote new policy narratives, entrepreneurship and competitiveness in particular. Through these new narratives new values and modes of action are installed and legitimated and new forms of moral authority are established and others are diminished or derided' (Ball, 2008: 24).

The third of Ball's processes of public sector transformation is flexibilization, where a plethora of approaches to teachers' conditions of service were legitimated, a new tier of teaching assistants was introduced into schools, and new systems for training teachers (to compete with existing and well-established forms) were introduced. The fourth process is destatization and destabilization. Ball explains this as the 'introduction of new providers by contracting-out of services, programmes and policy work, drastically blurring the already fuzzy divide between the public and private sectors' (Ball, 2008: 26). The last of Ball's processes of public sector transformation is, perhaps paradoxically, that of centralization. This was manifested in the retention of a national curriculum, albeit that large parts of the sector were allowed to opt out; in the continuing central funding and governance of certain types of schools; and in the creation with substantial powers of an inspection service to act as an enforcer of government policy, which rapidly became known as a standards and quality agenda.

Truth politics

Our relationship with the truth is changing. On the campaign trail to become President of the United States, Donald Trump took this relationship to new and unique places. When he claimed that Hillary Clinton, the Democratic candidate for the presidency, was responsible for the 'birther conspiracy', he wasn't only lying or being disingenuous, he was exploiting the power available to him as a result of this new relationship with the truth. This is different from a politician being permissive with the definition of truth. Kellyanne Conway, special advisor to President Trump, has talked of 'alternative facts'; the approach was also seen in the discourses on offer during the UK referendum on membership of the European Union (EU). Michael Gove, UK Member of Parliament and campaigner to leave the EU, said during the referendum: 'the British people are sick and tired of experts'. Since being elected, President Trump has intensified his attacks on the mainstream media and raised the spectre of false news when he doesn't like a story or a reporter.

Mark Zuckerberg, founder and CEO of Facebook, at first dismissed the power of false news, saying: 'to think it [fake news] influenced the election in any way is a pretty crazy idea' (Zuckerberg quoted in Newton, 2016). We have subsequently seen the rise of fake news, not least because President Trump exploits the power of the concept in support of his own agenda. The opinions of Zuckerberg appear to have become more nuanced over time, with Facebook now committed to a fight against so-called fake news. This raises an important issue for Facebook and all new media companies: what responsibilities do they have for the content on their sites? Companies like Facebook are forcefully resistant to the idea that they are media companies, defining themselves as merely platforms. They do this to avoid taking responsibility for the content on their sites. This ignores the value they add to the content. They professionalize the opinions of laypeople and with it bestow a level of unearned legitimacy.

This was again evident during the US presidential election. Edgar Maddison Welch walked into the Comet Ping Pong restaurant in Washington D.C. with a firearm, claiming to be self-investigating reports that Hillary Clinton was running a child sex ring out of the pizza restaurant. Welch fired the gun into the floor of the restaurant and was subsequently arrested without further incident. He was responding to a story that had already been widely discredited. This is evidence of the extraordinary ways in which how we understand and interact with the world are changing. This was a conspiracy theory with no credible source, no credible institution behind it, and no credible author, that acquired enough legitimacy to motivate an armed attack in a pizza restaurant.

Previously the privilege to publish had to be earned; one had to acquire a certified qualification, a job with a respected organization, or a contract with a publishing company. When these were acquired the individual was rewarded with the ear of the listener; his or her opinion carried more weight. The reader, through a type of branding or a respected publishing company logo on the paper, is able to identify this authority. When that brand is superseded by the Facebook brand we are left with no obvious way of differentiating the expert from the layperson.

We no longer live in a world with filters; the producers of content can no longer be described as experts, or at least we have no immediate way of working out their level of expertise. There are no longer any hurdles to be jumped over to get one's voice heard; anyone with an email address is a journalist these days. This move away from deferral to the expert is evidenced in the changing nature of our relationship with text and the production of content. The idea of democracy requires us to defer to experts. We elect our public officials not as experts themselves but because we accept we cannot be experts with regard to everything in the world; we cannot hold relevant opinions on everything. We trust our elected officials to listen to experts and make informed decisions. Increasingly this isn't the way people behave in the world. People rarely say that they simply do not have enough knowledge about a subject to form an opinion about it. And then they can always Google it, and trust in the sources they find. We have a view on everything and that view is encouraged and supported by our contact group.

This is particularly evident in the realm of public policy, where people have always had strong opinions on most things. Tom Nichols, Professor of National Security Affairs at the US Naval War College, described in an article in the journal *Foreign Affairs* how he has seen a 'Google-fuelled, Wikipedia-based, blog-sodden collapse of any division between professionals and laypeople, teachers and students, knowers and wonderers' (Nichols, 2017: n.p.). While people still defer to doctors they feel emboldened, in some cases, to question such important matters as vaccinations. This is an unprecedented questioning of authority and one that raises significant questions about how the world is organized.

Nichols describes an America that no longer wants to have a conversation about the validity of its ideas, but rather wants to have their ideas accepted because of the weight of emotional investment they place on those ideas. This tendency is being exploited by politicians in ways that we haven't seen before. In an extraordinary interview on CNN during the US election campaign, Newt Gingrich, former speaker of the US House of Representatives, was discussing violent crime in America, which it is widely acknowledged was declining. During the interview Gingrich said the following:

> Current view is that liberals have a whole set of statistics that theoretically may be right but they are not what human beings believe. ..... The average American, I will bet you this morning, does not *think* that crime is down, does not *think* we are safer ..... people *feel* more threatened. As a political candidate I'll go with what people feel.
>
> (Gingrich quoted in Johns, 2016; our italics)

It is extraordinary to hear a surrogate for a presidential candidate so publicly take this approach to facts and to the truth.

This type of politics is not happening in isolation. New media, in particular the Internet, is acting to reconfigure the relationship between producers and consumers of content. The role of the reader is, in some cases, changing from its traditional passive function to a more active and engaged role. The Internet has given the public the possibility of a more democratic relationship to the power of textual production, so that they are now in a more influential position in relation to content. The implications for society of myriad texts and myriad types and instances of textual readings can be said to have the effect of democratizing power, moving it away from the traditional holders like governments or the media and giving it to the people. Among the other implications of this democratization is the undermining of the expert. The expansion of the sources from which we gain knowledge leaves us in a difficult situation when it comes to deciding what to believe. Combined with the narrative of the lack of trust in our politicians, journalists, and experts, we are left with an overwhelming sea of noise. We have discarded our filters, or more accurately we have actively undermined those filters.

While it is very difficult to define exactly what we mean by truth it does appear that the post-truth discourse in politics is moving us further away from the reality of our lives. The Internet, understood in its widest sense, has played the defining role in changing the nature of this relationship over the last twenty years. Many of us use text in a different way; we hold immediate conversations through messaging apps, we blog, we tweet, and some of our most important relationships are defined by Facebook. Whereas previously the spoken word was the default mode of communication the new generation are using text more often.

This change in the way we produce and consume information, when combined with the greater importance of the written word as a more immediate communication technique, is having an impact on how we see the world. The difficulty of verifying information has resulted in the much discussed 'bubble' phenomenon: we only ever take in information that supports our worldview. This endless reinforcement of our own ideas is confirmation bias run riot. In its traditional form confirmation bias works as a filter of facts that we don't really like; it is powerful but remains a bias. This new world of information bubbles means our confirmation bias no longer has much work to do. There are no nasty facts that we need to filter out; everything we see already confirms our worldview.

This may act as some kind of comfort blanket for people and society but results in overwhelming shocks when the real world cannot be kept out of our bubbles. We have already referred to Brexit, and the election of Donald Trump as President of the United States, but these are likely high-profile examples of a phenomenon reaching deeper into the collective psyche. The bubbles we live in have always existed. We have always surrounded ourselves with like-minded people and been drawn to those who generally agree with us, but we have seen and understood other people's points of view. We have been able to empathize. The Internet has turned these transparent bubbles opaque.

An alternative approach to describing the world would seek to deconstruct texts and textual readings, by questioning: the use of binary oppositions which marginalize some forms of life at the expense of others (e.g. male/female, black/white, abled/dis-abled, heterosexual/homosexual, and classed binaries), the attachment of evaluations to particular words or phrases (e.g. one of the pair of words is given a greater value than the other, with a fairly obvious example (from a race discourse) being that white is privileged over black; in a gendered discourse, male is given a higher valuation than female; dis-ability is understood as inferior to ability, and so on), and the construction of boundaries around forms of thinking which act to exclude and marginalize people and other ideas.

This way of thinking is underpinned by a HyperTextual model of representation, in which the introduction of new media – in particular the Internet – is acting to reconfigure discursive arrangements and the place of the reader within them. Conventional models of textual production and consumption, that is, books and newspapers, have privileged the writer over the reader. The Internet has given us the possibility, though it is as yet hardly a revolution, of a more democratic relationship to the power of textual production, so that we are now in a more influential and powerful position in relation to texts and facts. (Look at the power of social media in influencing opinion; perhaps especially in elections such as the recent United States presidential election.)

This has been described as the HyperTextual dissolution of centrality, and what it means is that new media allow the possibility of conversation rather than instruction so that no one ideology, agenda, or viewpoint dominates any other. The HyperText author combines the function of both the reader and the writer. They merge with each other and become intertwined. This means that no longer does the reader simply absorb the contents of a written text; they now have the potentiality to influence what they read and more importantly how they read it.

This comprises the merging of what has historically been two very different processes. Today when we consider reading and writing, we probably think of them as serial processes or as procedures carried out intermittently by the same person: first one reads, then one writes, and then one reads some more. HyperText, which allows the possibility of having access to an almost infinite number of different texts produced by different authors, leads to an active reader, and in doing so infringes on the power of the writer, removing some of it and granting it to the reader.

Roland Barthes, the French structuralist, coined the terms, 'readerly' (in French, 'lisible') and 'writerly' (in French, 'scriptable'). These distinguish between two types of texts, and thus compel readers to interpret them (i.e. make sense of them) in very different ways. In the first case, the readerly text is read in a conventional way, with the authority of the text residing in what is being read. The reader has very little scope to interpret the text in ways other than those intended by the author. Barthes contrasts this with a writerly text and thus correspondingly a writerly way of reading that text, where the reader, in his or her reading of that text, is able to create meanings from that text which do not necessarily conform to the intentions of the author. He wrote as follows:

> The writerly text is a perpetual present, upon which no *consequent* language (which would inevitably make it past) can be superimposed; the writerly text is *ourselves writing*, before the infinite play of the world (the world as function) is traversed, intersected, stopped, plasticized by some singular system (Ideology, Genus, Criticism) which reduces the plurality of entrances, the opening of networks, the infinity of languages.
>
> (Barthes, 1975: 5)

This type of text and way of reading texts is more likely to be found on the Internet and through the use of the Internet (through processes such as HyperTextualization, a lack of control by official bodies, such as governments, and not reading these texts in a straightforward, linear way). The goal and purpose of reading texts in this way (i.e. through the Internet) is to make the reader no longer a consumer of textual information but a producer of such information.

The key concept that we have used in this book is difference; that is, the type and extent of dissimilarity between different manifestations of the categories, for example abled and dis-abled, men and women, black and white, heterosexual and homosexual, intelligent and unintelligent, precariat and middle class. Crude versions of these relations are ever-present in modern societies. However, difference can be understood in a number of ways. There is the common use given to the term, where difference is understood as not being or as being opposite to something else. Then there is the meaning given to the term by Jacques Derrida. In his 1982 essay 'Différance', he suggests that the term points to a number of ways that textual meaning can be produced. The first of these relates to the idea that words and signs have meaning only within other arrangements of words and concepts, from which they differ. This is the predominant way that we have used the idea of difference in this book, a use that has been sadly neglected in most discussions of equalities and inequalities. Meanings are thus forever deferred. The second way that Derrida uses the term is to refer to a notion of *espacement* or spacing, so that what should concern the investigator is the force that differentiates social elements from other social elements, and in the process – as we have suggested – engenders binary oppositions and endlessly reiterated hierarchies of meaning.

References

Ainscow, M. (2016) *Struggles for Equity in Education: The selected works of Mel Ainscow*. London: Routledge.

Alexander, R.J., Craft, M. and Lynch, J. (eds) (1984) *Change in Teacher Education: Context and provision since Robbins*. London: Holt, Rinehart and Winston.

Allan, J. (2008) *Rethinking Inclusive Education: The philosophers of difference in practice*. Dordrecht: Springer.

Anderson, M.J. (2009) *Carl Linnaeus: Father of classification*. Rev. ed. Berkeley Heights, NJ: Enslow.

Andrews, J., Hutchinson, J. and Johnnes, R. (2016) *Grammar Schools and Social Mobility*. London: Education Policy Institute.

Anemone, R.L. (2011) *Race and Human Diversity: A biocultural approach*. Upper Saddle River, NJ: Prentice Hall.

Ball, S.J. (2008) *The Education Debate*. Bristol: The Policy Press.

Barber, M., Mourshed, M. and McKinsey and Company (2007) *How the World's Best Performing Systems Come Out on Top*. London and New York: McKinsey.

Barnard, H.C. (1961) *A History of English Education from 1760*. London: University of London Press.

Barthes, R. (1975) *S/Z*. Trans. Miller, R. London: Jonathan Cape.

Bernstein, B. (2000) *Pedagogy, Symbolic Control and Identity: Theory, research and critique* (revised ed.). London: Rowman and Littlefield.

Bhaskar, R. (2011) *Reclaiming Reality: A critical introduction to contemporary philosophy*. New ed. London: Routledge.

Bhaskar, R. and Danermark, B. (2006) 'Metatheory, interdisciplinarity and disability research: A critical realist perspective'. *Scandinavian Journal of Disability Research*, 8 (4), 278–97.

Board of Education (1903) *Regulations for the Instruction and Training of Pupil-Teachers and Students in Training Colleges*. London: HMSO.

— (1904) *Regulations for the Training of Teachers and for the Examination of Students in Training Colleges*. London: HMSO.

— (1908) *Regulations for the Training of Teachers for Secondary Schools*. London: HMSO.

— (1909) *Report of the Board of Education for the Year 1907–1908*. London: HMSO.

— (1920) *Regulations for the Training of Teachers*. London: HMSO.

— (1921) *Draft Statutory Rules and Orders, Education, England, Training of Teachers (Amending) Regulations (No. 1), 1921*. London: HMSO.

— (1941) *Education after the War ("The Green Book")*. London: HMSO.

— (1943) *White Paper: Educational reconstruction*. London: HMSO.

Bolton, P. (2016) 'Grammar school statistics'. House of Commons Library Briefing Paper number 1398, 29 June 2016. Online. www.schoolzone.co.uk/schools/NCres/Grammar_school_statistics.pdf (accessed 8 October 2017).

Booth, T. and Ainscow, M. (2011) *The Index for Inclusion*. Bristol: Studies in Inclusive Education.

Boswell, J. (1980) *Christianity, Social Tolerance, and Homosexualit[y]* University of Chicago Press.

Boudon, R. (1973) *Education, Opportunity and Social Inequality*. N[ew York:] John Wiley.

Bourdieu, P. (1986) 'The forms of capital'. In Richardson, J.G. (ed.) *Handbook of Theory and Research for the Sociology of Education*. New York: Greenwood Press, 241–58.

Bourdieu, P. and Passeron, J.-C. (1977) *Reproduction in Education, Society and Culture*. Trans. Nice, R. London: SAGE Publications.

Bowles, S. and Gintis, H. (1976) *Schooling in Capitalist America: Educational reform and the contradictions of economic life*. New York: Basic Books.

British Dyslexia Association (n.d.) 'What are specific learning difficulties?' Online. www.bdadyslexia.org.uk/educator/what-are-specific-learning-difficulties (accessed 28 September 2017).

British Psychological Society (1999) *Dyslexia, Literacy and Psychological Assessment*. Report of the Working Party of the DECP of British Psychological Society (BPS). London: BPS.

Brown, A., Fleetwood, S. and Roberts, J.M. (eds) (2002) *Critical Realism and Marxism*. London: Routledge.

Chitty, C. (2004) *Education Policy in Britain*. Basingstoke: Palgrave Macmillan.

Chitty, C. and Dunford, J. (eds) (1999) *State Schools: New Labour and the Conservative legacy*. London: Woburn Press.

Clarendon Commission (2004) *The Clarendon Report: English public schools in the nineteenth century*. Originally 1864. Bristol: Thoemmes Continuum.

Clarke, K. (1991) 'Speech to Conservative Party Conference, September', cited in *Department of Education and Science Bulletin*, 362/91. London: Department of Education and Science.

Coe, R. and Tymms, P. (2008) 'Summary of research on changes in educational standards in the UK', in M. Harris (ed.), *Education Briefing Book 2008: IoD Policy Paper*. London: Institute of Directors.

Committee on Higher Education (1963) *Higher Education: Report of the Committee appointed by the Prime Minister under the Chairmanship of Lord Robbins, 1961–63*. London: HMSO.

Daly, M. (1992) *Outercourse: The be-dazzling voyage, containing recollections from my Logbook of a Radical Feminist Philosopher (be-ing an account of my time/space travels and ideas – then, again, now, and how)*. San Francisco: HarperSanFrancisco.

Dearing, R. (1993) *The National Curriculum and its Assessment: Interim report (the Dearing Report)*. London: Schools Examinations and Assessment Council and NCC.

— (1994) *The National Curriculum and its Assessment – Full report (the Dearing Report)*. London: Schools Examinations and Assessment Council and NCC.

Dent, H.C. (1977) *The Training of Teachers in England and Wales, 1800–1975*. London: Hodder and Stoughton.

Derrida, J. (1982) 'Différance'. In Derrida, J. *Margins of Philosophy*. Trans. Bass, A. Chicago: University of Chicago Press, 1–28.

DES (Department of Education and Science) (1965) *Circular 10/65: The organization of secondary education*. London: HMSO.

— (1972a) *Education: A framework for expansion*. London: HMSO.

— (1972b) *Teacher Education and Training: Report by a Committee of Inquiry appointed by the Secretary of State for Education and Science, under the Chairmanship of Lord James of Rusholme*. London: HMSO.

— (1977) *Education in Schools: A consultative document*. London: HMSO.

— (1983) 'School standards and spending: statistical analysis'. *Statistical Bulletin* 16/83. London: HMSO.

— (1984) 'School standards and spending: statistical analysis: a further appreciation'. *Statistical Bulletin* 13/84. London: HMSO.

— (1988a) *Task Group on Testing and Assessment: A report*. London: HMSO.

— (1988b) *Three Supplementary Reports to TGAT*. London: HMSO.

Devine, F. (2004) *Class Practices: How parents help their children get good jobs*. Cambridge: Cambridge University Press.

DfE (Department for Education) (1992) *Circular 1992: Initial Teacher Training (Secondary Phase)*. Department for Education/Welsh Office, London.

— (1994) *SEN Code of Practice*. London: HMSO.

— (2015) *Policy Paper. 2010 to 2015 government policy: academies and free schools*. London: HMSO.

— (2016a) 'SFR01/2016: Revised GCSE and equivalent results in England 2014/15'. Online. www.gov.uk/government/uploads/system/uploads/attachment_data/file/494052/SFR01_2016_National_Tables.xlsx (accessed 27 September 2017).

— (2016b) 'SFR20/2016: Special educational needs in England: January 2016'. Online. www.gov.uk/government/statistics/special-educational-needs-in-england-january-2016 (accessed 8 October 2017).

— (2016c) *Schools, Pupils and their Characteristics: January 2016*. Online. www.gov.uk/government/uploads/system/uploads/attachment_data/file/532038/SFR20_2016_National_Tables.xlsx (accessed 23 November 2017).

DfEE (Department for Education and Employment) (1992) *White Paper: Choice and Diversity*. London: HMSO.

— (1996) *Graduate Teacher Programme: Consultation paper*. London: Department for Education and Employment.

— (1998) *Teaching: High status, high standards: Requirements for courses of initial teacher training* (Circular 4/98). London: Department for Education and Employment.

DfES (Department for Education and Skills) (2001) *Special Educational Needs: Code of Practice*. London: HMSO.

Dyson, A., Goldrick, S., Jones, L. and Kerr, K. (2010) *Equity in Education: Creating a fairer education system: A manifesto for the reform of education in England*. Manchester: Centre for Equity in Education.

The Economist (2016) 'The post-truth world: Yes, I'd lie to you'. *The Economist*, 10 September. Online. www.economist.com/news/briefing/21706498-dishonesty-politics-nothing-new-manner-which-some-politicians-now-lie-and (accessed 19 August 2017).

Edge, K. (2001) 'School-Based Management: Q&A for the web/knowledge nugget'. World Bank Decentralization & SBM Resource Kit. Washington, DC: World Bank. Online. http://web.worldbank.org/archive/website00238I/WEB/PDF/SBMQ_AF.PDF (accessed 28 September 2017).

Education Commission (1861) *Report of the Commissioners Appointed to Inquire into the State of Popular Education in England* (Vol. 1). London: HMSO.

— (1888) *Final Report of the Commissioners Appointed to Inquire into the Elementary Education Acts, England and Wales.* London: HMSO.

Education Datalab (2016) *Understanding Grammar Schools.* Philip Nye, Education Datalab. Online. http://educationdatalab.org.uk (accessed 2 January 2018).

Education Department (1890) *Education Department Minute of 10th March 1890, Establishing a New Code of Regulations, by the Right Honourable the Lords of the Committee of the Privy Council on Education.* London: HMSO.

— (1898) *Report of the Departmental Committee on the Pupil-Teacher System* (Vol. 1). London: HMSO.

Fairclough, N. (2000) *New Labour, New Language?* London: Routledge.

Flax, J. (1990) *Thinking Fragments: Psychoanalysis, feminism, and postmodernism in the contemporary West.* Berkeley: University of California Press.

Ford, L. (2007) 'Tories abandon grammar schools.' *The Guardian,* 16 May. Online. www.theguardian.com/education/2007/may/16/schools.grammarschools (accessed 28 September 2017).

Foucault, M. (1979) *Discipline and Punish: The birth of the prison.* Trans. Sheridan, A. New York: Vintage Books.

— (1988) *The History of Sexuality: The care of the self.* Trans. Hurley, R. New York: Vintage Books. Vol. 3 of *The History of Sexuality.* 3 vols. 1988–90.

— (1990a) *The History of Sexuality: An introduction.* Trans. Hurley, R. New York: Vintage Books. Vol. 1 of *The History of Sexuality.* 3 vols. 1988–90.

— (1990b) *The History of Sexuality: The use of pleasure.* Trans. Hurley, R. New York: Vintage Books. Vol. 2 of *The History of Sexuality.* 3 vols. 1988–90.

Furlong, J. (2005) 'New Labour and teacher education: The end of an era'. *Oxford Review of Education,* 31 (1), 119–34.

Ghosh, P. and Goldman, L. (eds) (2006) *Politics and Culture in Victorian Britain: Essays in memory of Colin Matthew.* Oxford: Oxford University Press.

Griffin, S. (2000) *Woman and Nature: The roaring inside her.* San Francisco: Sierra Club Books.

Hacking, I. (1990) *The Taming of Chance.* Cambridge: Cambridge University Press.

Hayes, E. and Nimis, S. (2011) *Plutarch's Dialogue on Love: An intermediate Greek reader.* Oxford, OH: Faenum Publishing.

Hearnshaw, L.S. (1979) *Cyril Burt: Psychologist.* Ithaca, NY: Cornell University Press.

hooks, b. (1982) *Ain't I a Woman: Black women and feminism.* London: Pluto Press.

House of Commons (2003) *Secondary Education: Diversity of Provision.* London: Education and Skills Committee, House of Commons.

Hyams, B.K. (1979) 'Anti-intellectualism in the history of the education of teachers: England and Australia'. *Journal of Educational Administration and History*, 11 (1), 43–9.

Independent Schools Association (2016) *ISC Census and Annual Report 2016*. London: Independent Schools Council. Online. www.isc.co.uk/media/3179/isc_census_2016_final.pdf (accessed 11 January 2018).

— (2017) *ISC Census and Annual Report 2017*. London: Independent Schools Council. Online. www.isc.co.uk/media/4069/isc-census-2017-final.pdf (accessed 11 January 2018).

Jesson, D. (2013) *The Creation, Development and Present State of Grammar Schools in England*. York: Centre for Performance Evaluation and Resource Management.

Johns, C. (2016) 'Damned lies and statistics in a post-truth world'. *The Irish Times*, 13 August. www.irishtimes.com/opinion/damned-lies-and-statistics-in-a-post-truth-world-1.2754474 (accessed 27 September 2017).

Kent County Council (2017) *Familiarisation Booklet*. Online. https://www.kent.gov.uk/__data/assets/pdf_file/0014/14513/Kent-Test-familiarisation-booklet.pdf (accessed 2 January 2018).

Ladson-Billings, G. and Tate, W.F. (1995) 'Toward a critical race theory of education'. *Teachers College Record*, 97 (1), 47–68.

Lancaster, J. (1803) *Improvements in Education, as It Respects the Industrious Classes of the Community: Containing, a short account of its present state, hints towards its improvement, and a detail of some practical experiments conducive to that end*. London: Darton and Harvey.

— (1807) *Improvements in Education, as It Respects the Industrious Classes of the Community: Containing, among other important particulars, an account of the Institution for the Education of One Thousand Poor Children, Borough Road, Southwark; and of the new system of education on which it is conducted, to which is prefixed a sketch of the New-York Free School*. New York: Collins and Perkins.

Leach, A.F. (1915) *The Schools of Medieval England*. London: Methuen.

Long, R. and Bolton, P. (2017) 'Faith Schools in England: FAQs'. House of Commons Library briefing paper 06972, 13 March 2017. Online. http://researchbriefings.files.parliament.uk/documents/SN06972/SN06972.pdf (accessed 8 October 2017).

Marks, J., Cox, C. and Pomian-Srzednicki, M. (1983) *Standards in English Schools*. London: NCES.

Marx, K. and Engels, F. (2004) *The Communist Manifesto*. Originally 1848. London: Penguin Books.

McNair, A. (1944) *Teachers and Youth Leaders: Report of the Committee appointed by the President of the Board of Education to consider the supply, recruitment and training of teachers and youth leaders*. London: HMSO.

Meads, J. (1998) 'A Grammar School Education Between the Wars'. *Audley Historian* 4. Online. http://www.audleyfhs.co.uk/Journal%204/A%20Grammer%20School%20Education.htm (accessed 2 January 2018).

Messick, S. (1989) 'Validity'. In Linn, R. (ed.) *Educational Measurement*. 3rd ed. Washington, D.C.: American Council on Education.

Ministry of Education (1945) *The Nation's Schools: Their plans and purposes* (Ministry of Education Pamphlet No. 1). London: HMSO.

— (1947) *The New Secondary Education* (Ministry of Education Pamphlet No. 9). London: HMSO.

Ministry of Education, New Zealand (2011) *Targeted Funding for Educational Achievement*. Wellington: Ministry of Education.

Newton, C. (2016) 'Zuckerberg: The idea that fake news on Facebook influenced the election is "crazy"'. *The Verge*, 10 November. www.theverge.com/2016/11/10/13594558/mark-zuckerberg-election-fake-news-trump (accessed 27 September 2017).

Nichols, T. (2017) 'How America lost faith in expertise: And why that's a giant problem'. *Foreign Affairs*, March/April, 96 (2). Online. www.foreignaffairs.com/articles/united-states/2017-02-13/how-america-lost-faith-expertise (accessed 19 August 2017).

Norwood, C. (1943) *Curriculum and Examinations in Secondary Schools: Report of the Committee of the Secondary School Examinations Council appointed by the President of the Board of Education in 1941*. London: HMSO.

OECD (Organisation for Economic Co-operation and Development) (2010a) *Closing the Gap for Immigrant Students: Policies, practice and performance* (OECD Reviews of Migrant Education). Paris: OECD.

— (2010b) *Education at a Glance 2010: OECD indicators*. Paris: OECD. Online. www.oecd.org/edu/eag2010 (accessed 20 April 2011).

— (2011) *Education at a Glance 2011: OECD indicators*. Paris: OECD.

— (2015) *Education Policy Outlook 2015: Making reforms happen*. Paris: OECD.

Office for National Statistics (2015) 'Household disposable income and inequality'. Online. http://webarchive.nationalarchives.gov.uk/20160128172042/http://www.ons.gov.uk/ons/rel/household-income/household-disposable-income-and-inequality/index.html (accessed 8 October 2017).

Omi, M. and Winant, H. (1994) *Racial Formation in the United States: From the 1960s to the 1990s*. 2nd ed. New York: Routledge.

Osberg, D. and Biesta, G. (2007) 'Beyond presence: epistemological and pedagogical implications of strong emergence'. *Interchange*, 38 (1): 31–51.

Patten, J. (1992). 'Who's afraid of the "s" word?' *New Statesman and Society*, 17 July, 20–1.

Peel, M. (2015) *The New Meritocracy: A history of UK independent schools, 1979–2015*. London: Elliott and Thompson.

Reid, G. (2011) *Dyslexia: A practitioner's handbook*. London, New York: Continuum.

Reiss, M. and Brooks, G. (2004) *Developmental Dyslexia in Adults: A research review*. London: National Research and Development Centre.

Rizvi, F. and Lingard, B. (2010) *Globalizing Education Policy*. London: Routledge.

Rutherford, A. (2014) 'He may have unravelled DNA, but James Watson deserves to be shunned'. *The Guardian*, 1 December. Online. www.theguardian.com/commentisfree/2014/dec/01/dna-james-watson-scientist-selling-nobel-prize-medal (accessed 19 August 2017).

Schleicher, A. (2015) 'Seven big myths about top-performing school systems.' *BBC News*, 4 February. Online. www.bbc.co.uk/news/business-31087545 (accessed 28 September 2017).

Schön, D.A. (1983) *The Reflective Practitioner: How professionals think in action.* New York: Basic Books.

Scott, D. (2011) *Education, Epistemology and Critical Realism.* London: Routledge.

— (2017) *Education Systems and Learners: Knowledge and knowing.* London: Palgrave Macmillan.

School Examinations and Assessment Council (SEAC) (1989a) *National Curriculum Assessment Arrangements (1).* London: SEAC.

— (1989b) *National Curriculum Assessment Arrangements (2).* London: SEAC.

Sen, A. (1985) *Commodities and Capabilities.* Amsterdam: North-Holland.

Slee, R. (2010) *The Irregular School: Exclusion, schooling and inclusive education.* London: Routledge.

Smyth, J. (2001) 'Critical reflection: The antidote to being done to!' in J. Smyth (ed.) *Critical Politics of Teachers' Work: An Australian Perspective*, New York: Peter Lang, 183–96.

Social Mobility and Child Poverty Commission (2014) *Elitist Britain?* Online. www.gov.uk/government/publications/elitist-britain (accessed 28 September 2017).

Social Mobility Commission (2016) *State of the Nation 2016: Social mobility in Great Britain.* Online. www.gov.uk/government/publications/state-of-the-nation-2016 (accessed 2 January 2018).

SPCK (Society for Promoting Christian Knowledge) (1711) *An Account of Charity-Schools in Great Britain and Ireland.* 10th ed. London: Joseph Downing.

Spens, W. (1938) *Report of the Consultative Committee on Secondary Education with Special Reference to Grammar Schools and Technical High Schools.* London: HMSO.

Stobart, G. (2008) *Testing Times: The uses and abuses of assessment.* London: Routledge.

Taunton Commission (1868) *Report on the State of Education.* UK government.

Taylor, C. (2007) *A Secular Age.* Cambridge, MA: Harvard University Press.

UNESCO (United Nations Educational, Scientific and Cultural Organization) (1994) *The Salamanca Statement and Framework for Action on Special Needs Education.* Online. www.unesco.org/education/pdf/SALAMA_E.PDF (accessed 28 September 2017). Paris: UNESCO.

— (2009) *Policy Guidelines on Inclusion in Education.* Paris: UNESCO.

— (n.d.) 'UIS statistics'. http://data.uis.unesco.org/ (accessed 8 October 2017).

UNICEF (United Nations Children's Fund) (2007) *Child Poverty in Perspective: An overview of child well-being in rich countries: A comprehensive assessment of the lives and well-being of children and adolescents in the economically advanced nations* (Innocenti Report Card 7). Florence: UNICEF Innocenti Research Centre.

Van der Meer, F. (1961) *Augustine the Bishop: The life and work of a father of the church.* London: Sheed and Ward.

Vernon, P.E. (ed.) (1957) *Secondary School Selection: A British Psychological Society inquiry.* London: Methuen.

Warnock, H.M. (1978) *Special Educational Needs: Report of the Committee of Enquiry into the Education of Handicapped Children and Young People.* London: HMSO.

Weber, M. (2013) *The Protestant Ethic and the Spirit of Capitalism.* Originally 1904–5. CreateSpace Independent Publishing Platform.

Wikipedia (2012) 'File:Grammar school ballots in England.svg'. Map derived by Kanguole from 'English administrative divisions 2010' by Nilfanion. Online. https://commons.wikimedia.org/wiki/File:Grammar_school_ballots_in_England. svg (accessed 11 January 2018).

Wiliam, D. (2011) *Embedded Formative Assessment.* Bloomington, IN: Solution Tree Press.

Wilkinson, R. and Pickett, K. (2009) *The Spirit Level: Why more equal societies almost always do better.* London: Allen Lane.

Williams, R. (1961) *The Long Revolution.* London: Chatto and Windus.

Yates, A. and Pidgeon, D.A. (1957) *Admission to Grammar Schools.* London: Newnes.

Index

A

academy converter 80, 81, 85
accountability 39, 57, 65, 89–90, 94–7, 100, 119, 132, 136–8, 140
acquisition 18–19
agency 56, 96
Ainscow, M. 135, 137
Alexander, R. 53
Allan, J. 13, 80
ancient history 33
Anderson, M. 4
Anemone, R. 12
arithmetic 31, 71, 72, 73
arthrogryposis 106
assessment 15, 27, 65, 77, 87, 90–105, 113, 115, 118–19, 123, 130, 139
autonomy 53–4, 85, 88

B

Bachelor of Education (BEd) 51, 54, 56
Ball, S. 89, 140–1
Barber, M. 105
Barnard, H. 47
Barthes, R. 145–6
behaviour 4, 6, 16, 36, 46, 79, 106–7, 110, 115, 124–6, 127
Bernstein, B. 111
Bhaskar, R. 13, 22, 28–30
Biesta, G. 128
binary opposition 6–8, 127, 129, 147
black paper 65
Board of Education 48, 50, 59, 62
Bolton, P. 66, 69, 81, 82
Booth, T. 137
Boswell, J. 17
Boudon, R. 63
Bourdieu, P. 39, 40, 42, 133
Bowles, S. 133
British Dyslexia Association 109–10
Brooks, G. 109
Brown, A. 30
bureaucracy 99
bursary system 48

C

capital 18, 19, 39, 63, 135; cultural 40; material 40; social 40
case 56, 113, 123
change 3, 4, 6, 22–4, 27, 29, 45, 88–90, 127–9
chaos 139–40
charity 33, 36, 46, 85
Charity Commission 37
Charity Tribunal 37

Chitty, C. 60
Christianity 16, 38, 46–54
City Technology College 78, 140
Clarendon Commission 34, 38; Report 34, 38
Clarke, K. 54, 96, 97
classification 38, 65
Coe, R. 99
Committee on Higher Education 51
communication 46, 108, 144
community 5, 9, 11, 26, 60, 85, 88, 132, 135–9
competence 54, 88, 102
complexity theory 46, 127–9
comprehensive 14, 60–1, 64–7, 79, 134
concept x, 2, 3, 5–8, 10, 30, 101, 105, 146–7
confession 122–6
construct 12, 13–15, 86, 102–3, 112, 122, 123, 125, 127, 129, 131, 135, 144
content 2, 44, 45, 46, 89, 100, 111, 138, 142–5
contradiction 5, 10, 15, 99
control 9, 11, 88, 89, 90, 96, 98, 100, 111–13
craft knowledge 44–6
critical race theory 9, 12
Cross Commission 49
culture 13, 19, 27, 32, 38, 39, 103, 105, 132, 133, 136
curriculum 33–4, 38–40, 60–1, 79, 81, 85, 89–101, 104, 111–13, 119, 130, 133, 136, 141; Augustinian 31; ideologies 38–40; integration 11–13; Latinate 31–2

D

Daly, M. 9
Danermark, B. 13
Dearing Report (2007) 97
Dearing, R. 91–9
democratic education 129, 143
Dent, H. 52
Department for Education 57, 78, 79, 85, 106, 107, 116, 118, 119
Department of Education and Science 14, 54, 85, 118, 121
Derrida, J. 146–7
determinacy x, 8, 14, 24, 46, 92
Devine, F. 19
dialogue 16, 46, 125
difference 1–30, 146–7
dis-ability 1–30, 106–39
discourse 5–8, 141–7
disposition 7, 8, 18, 27, 28, 101, 102, 103, 112
diversity 54, 80, 132–9
Dunford, J. 60
dyscalculia 108
dyslexia 108–9
Dyson, A. 136
dyspraxia 108

E
Edge, K.   137–8
Education (Schools) Act (1992)   54
Education Act   59–62, 63, 67
Education Commission (1988)   34–5
Education Department   47, 49
Education Reform Act, 1988, England
    and Wales   88
education girls'   15, 31, 34, 37–8;
    independent   31–43; private   31–43
effort   27–8
Elementary Education Act (1870)   34
eleven-plus test   13–15, 62, 64, 76–7
elitism   39
emergence   45, 128
Endowed Schools Act (1869)   34–5
Engels, F.   18
engineering   35, 37
English   32, 33, 34, 50, 71, 73, 78, 97
epistemology   11, 88
equilibrium   113
European Union   141
examination   88–105
exclusion   106–22, 127–39
Executive Technician   44–6

F
Fairclough, N.   86
fallibility   128
Fast Track Scheme   56–7
feedback   111–13
field of education   x, 2, 123
Finland   105, 134, 139
Flax, J.   10
Fleming Committee (1942)   36
Ford, L.   67
formal learning   13
formative assessment   91, 92, 93, 97, 98
Foucault, M.   122–6
foundationalism   4, 86, 104
Framing   x, 111–2
freedom   26, 85, 87
French   33, 34, 50, 145
function   6, 8, 26, 36, 45, 63, 80, 92, 94,
    98, 106, 108, 112, 113, 143, 145
Furlong, J.   55

G
gender   64, 8–12
General Certificate of Secondary Education
    (GCSE)   24, 25, 71, 96, 97, 99
generality   6–8, 127, 129
German   33, 34
Ghosh, P.   34
Gintis, H.   133
globalization   55, 138
Goldman, L.   34
Graduate Teacher Programme   55
grammar schools   62–87
Griffin, S.   10

H
Hacking, I.   127
Hayes, E.   16
Hearnshaw, L.   62
history   33, 34, 50, 97
holism   13, 136
hooks, b.   9
human mind   5, 14, 60, 64, 114, 115
humanism   38
Hyams, B.   50

I
identity   6, 124, 127, 139
implementation   27, 28, 47, 58, 119, 129,
    130, 131, 135
inclusive education   106–22, 127–39
Independent Schools Association
    40, 41, 42
Index for Inclusion   137
individualism   132
individuality in the field of
    documentation   123
industrial trainers   35
inequality   1–30, 87, 100–1, 135, 136, 139
instruction   35, 48, 60, 61, 145
intelligence   x, 2, 4, 5, 13–15, 19, 30, 60,
    62, 64, 77, 80, 81, 93, 108, 127
intentionality   7
interests   3, 46, 91, 110, 129, 130, 136
international comparisons   101, 104,
    110, 132, 133
intervention   87, 90, 91, 118, 119,
    134, 136, 140

J
James Committee (1971)   52–3
James Report (1971)   52–3
Jesson, D.   63
Johns, C.   143
judgement   29, 44, 77, 97, 98, 99, 104

K
knowledge   x, 2, 4, 6, 7, 8, 10, 11, 28–30,
    38, 39, 44–6, 47, 55, 62, 88, 98, 101–3,
    110–3, 122, 123, 125, 127

L
Ladson-Billings, G.   12
Lancaster, J.   47
Leach, A.   31
leadership   38, 57, 88
learning   6, 14, 22, 27–8, 33, 37, 44–6,
    61, 64–5, 79, 90–4, 100–14, 118, 119,
    134–7, 139, 140
legitimacy   6, 8, 14, 127, 129, 142
liberal education   34, 35
Lingard, B.   132
local education authority   61, 94, 107,
    114, 116, 117
Long, R.   81

Index

M

managerialism 89
Marx, K. 18
mathematics 33, 34, 37, 50, 76, 77, 79, 97
McNair, A. 51
meaning 2–3, 5, 7, 46, 64, 67,
105, 146, 147
mechanism x, 13, 28–30, 86, 90–1, 94,
99, 104, 105, 111, 122–3, 125–6, 128,
129, 139, 140
methodology 54, 101
Ministry of Education 62, 63, 137
model 1–30, 86, 90, 95, 97, 98, 99, 100,
104, 113, 129–39, 145
monitorial system 47
moral agent x, 10, 33, 60, 86, 89, 103, 140
Mourshed, M. 105

N

National Literacy Strategy 78
National Numeracy Strategy 78
Newcastle Report 34
Newton, C. 141
Nichols, T. 143
Nimis, S. 16
normalization 123
Norwood, C. 15

O

Object for a Branch of Knowledge 123
observation 3, 44, 99
Office for National Statistics (ONS) 23
Office for Standards in Education
(OFSTED) 54, 79, 89, 99, 131
old humanists 35
Omi, M. 12
ontology x, 28–9, 127, 128, 129
Organisation for Economic Co-operation
and Development (OECD) 101, 103,
105, 132, 134
Osberg, D. 128

P

participation 9, 100, 103, 107, 110, 119,
132, 133, 135, 139
Passeron, J.-C. 39, 133
pastoralism 39
Patten, J. 78
pedagogy 38, 90, 92, 110, 111
Peel, M. 33
performativity 6, 7, 8, 89, 127, 129
philosophy 10, 12, 32
Pickett, K. 133, 135, 136, 139
Pidgeon, D. 15
policy 92, 94; centrally directed
128–31; pluralist 128–31
politics truth x, 1–5, 141–7
Post-Graduate Certificate of
Education 52–7

power 1–5, 10, 11, 12, 14, 18, 30, 38,
39, 40, 79, 88, 96, 100, 120, 122–6,
127–31, 141–7
problem 4, 8, 9, 12, 14, 15, 18, 26, 49,
79, 86, 92, 96, 98, 103, 108, 128,
130, 134, 136
productive 18, 30; learning environments
92; practices 138
professional development 46, 56,
90, 100, 118
professionalism 55, 89, 95, 132, 137
Programme for International Student
Assessment (PISA) 101–5
progression 111–13
Public Schools Act (1868) 34

Q

Qualified Teacher Status (QTS) 54, 56, 57

R

race 3–4, 145
racial formation theory 12
rationality 5, 9, 10, 11, 55, 139
realism 38–40
reference 5–8, 32, 51, 91, 93, 94, 127, 129
reflection 44–6
reflective practitioner 44–6
reflexivity 46
reform 28, 47, 51–2, 88, 90–2, 99, 100,
132, 133–6, 140
regulation 48, 49, 50, 89, 100
Reid, G. 108
Reiss, M. 109
relational experience 9, 104
religious belief 32, 44–58
representation 63, 102, 127, 129, 141–7
repression 124
responsibility 33, 52, 86, 87, 142
rights 9, 10, 18, 133
Rizvi, F. 132
Rutherford, A. 4

S

Salamanca Statement (1994) 110–1
scaffolding 44
Schleicher, A. 101
Schön, D. 46
School Examinations and Assessment
Council 95–7
school academy 59–87; community
59–87; comprehensive 59–87;
direct-grant grammar 59–87;
effectiveness 37, 100–2; faith
80–2; free 59–87; foundation
59–87; government 59–87;
grammar 59–87; private 31–43;
secondary modern 59–87; studio
59–87; university training 59–87;
voluntary-aided 59–87; voluntary-
controlled 59–87
science 33, 34, 37, 50, 79, 80, 97, 105
Scott, D. 3, 8, 110, 127

secularism 32
selection 59–87
Sen, A. 26
separation 44
sexuality 16–7, 122–6
simulation 111
Slee, R. 135
Smyth, J. 88
Social Mobility and Child Poverty
    Commission 24–6
social integration 86
Society for Promoting Christian
    Knowledge 46
space 32, 45, 147
Special Educational Needs (SEN)
    12–3, 106–22
Spens, W. 15
standard 57, 65, 78, 98, 100, 101,
    119, 140, 141
Stobart, G. 102
summative assessment 92, 100
surveillance 122

T
Targeted Funding for Educational
    Achievement (TFEA) 138
Task Group on Assessment and Testing
    Report (1988) 90–6
Taunton Commission 34–5
taxonomy 38
Taylor, C. 32
Teach First, UK 57
teacher training 44–58
teaching profession 58, 88–9
technology 33, 89, 97, 103

testing 88–105
thinking 108, 139–40, 145
time 2, 6, 22, 113
training college 47–51
Training Development Agency for
    Schools 56
transfer 29, 45, 104
transformation 33, 65, 102, 132, 138, 140
tripartite system 13–4, 62, 65, 66
Tymms, P. 99

U
United Nations Educational, Scientific and
    Cultural Organisation (UNESCO)
    110–1, 132–3

V
value 2, 3, 6, 7, 8
Van der Meer, F. 16
Vernon, P. 15
visibility 122–3

W
Warnock Report (1978) 106, 113–8
Warnock, H. 113–8
Washback 90, 102, 104
Weber, M. 18
White Paper, *Educational Reconstruction*
    (1943) 59
Wilkinson, R. 133, 135, 136, 139
Williams, R. 32, 35, 38
Winant, H. 12

Y
Yates, A. 15

'What an important book and one that should worry us all. Thank goodness for truth-tellers like David and Ben.'

Professor Paul Gibbs, Centre for Education Research and Scholarship (CERS), Middlesex University

'A thoughtful and thought-provoking book. Essential reading for anyone who wants to understand how inequalities in the English education system have arisen and are perpetuated.'

Professor Carrie Paechter, Director, Nottingham Centre for Children, Young People and Families, Nottingham Trent University

'This is a brilliant book for anyone seeking to understand education in England today. Theoretically robust and forensic in its analysis, the authors have provided us with authoritative and richly illustrated accounts that are both informative and potentially transformative. David Scott and Ben Scott can be congratulated for writing a book that is both accessible and provocative. A self-avowed "work in progress", it is a warning against complacency.'

David Lambert, Professor of Geography Education, UCL Institute of Education